Anecdotes for Reflection

Part II

THE WORLD FEDERATION
OF KHOJA SHIA ITHNA-ASHERI MUSLIM COMMUNITIES
www.world-federation.org

بِسْمِ اللَّهِ الرَّحْمَٰنِ الرَّحِيمِ

In the Name of Allāh, the Most Gracious, the Most Merciful

FOREWORD

THE CONCEPT OF MORALITY has existed since the creation of mankind. In the old days, there was a clear distinction between 'good' morals and 'bad' morals although people did not always follow the former. During modern times, the distinction between good and bad has become blurred and morality has been significantly diluted. As a result, there is a danger that immorality will prevail over morality throughout the world.

There is no excuse for a Muslim to get caught in this quagmire. There is clear guidance from Allāh through Noble Qur'an and the Prophets and Maʿṣūmīn. Prophet Muḥammad ﷺ himself said, "I have been sent for the purpose of perfecting morals." One of the best ways of understanding morality is by studying practical examples from the lives of Prophets and Maʿṣūmīn.

A few books have been written on moral stories emanating from the Islāmic world, one of them being 'Pearls of Wisdom', published by the Islamic Education Board of World Federation in March 1993. Bearing in mind the importance of the subject of Akhlāqiyat, IEB-WF is publishing 'Anecdotes for Reflection' in 5 parts. The source of this publication is the book 'Yaksad Mawzu' wa 500 Dastan' by Sayyid Ali Akber Sadaqat. The translation from Farsi to English was carried out by Shaykh Shahnawaz Mahdavi. IEB – WF would like to thank Sayyid Ali Akber Sadaqat and Shaykh Shahnawaz Mahdavi for their efforts and we pray to Allāh ﷻ to reward them amply.

May Allāh ﷻ accept this work as a further attempt by IEB – WF to propagate Islām.

Islamic Education Board
The World Federation of K S I Muslim Communities
Muharram 1426 / February 2005

CONTENTS

TRANSLITERATION TABLE

The method of transliteration of Islāmic terminology from the ʿArabic language has been carried out according to the standard transliteration table mentioned below.

ء	ʾ	ض	ḍ
ا	a	ط	ṭ
ب	b	ظ	ẓ
ت	t	ع	ʿ
ث	th	غ	gh
ج	j	ف	f
ح	ḥ	ق	q
خ	kh	ك	k
د	d	ل	l
ذ	dh	م	m
ر	r	ن	n
ز	z	و	w
س	s	ي	y
ش	sh	ه	h
ص	ṣ		

Long Vowels		Short Vowels	
ا	ā	ـَـ	a
وَ	ū	ـُـ	u
ي	ī	ـِـ	i

سبحانه وتعالى Glory and Greatness be to Him - Used for Allāh

صلى الله عليه وآله Prayers be upon him and his family - Used for the Prophet Muḥammad

عليه السلام Peace be upon him - Used for noble personalities [Masculine]

عليها السلام Peace be upon her - Used for noble personalities [Feminine]

Introduction

THERE ARE NUMEROUS WAYS for man to achieve guidance and emerge from darkness and move towards light. Allāh ﷻ, for the prosperity of man and perfection of his morals, has created proofs, evidences and vestiges,[1] so great in number that they are beyond reckoning and computation. For the guidance of mankind, He sent the Prophets with clear proofs[2], books, miracles and signs so that, perhaps, the people might perceive the right path and attain prosperity and success.

During the entire period of his prophethood, the Noble Prophet ﷺ, with regards to refinement of souls and perfection of morals, was an exemplar in speech and deed, and had (even) said, "I have been sent (as a Prophet) for (the purpose of) perfecting the morals." [3]

Man's problem lies in his disregard for virtues, acquisition of vices, and inclination towards lust and obedience to Shaīṭān. Some men stoop so low that they even lead their lives akin to animals. For the purpose of refinement and treatment of human morals, abatement of rebelliousness and controlling the natural disposition, the Noble Prophet ﷺ spared no effort and mentioned all that was necessary in this regard.

Attainment of prosperity in this world and the Hereafter is only accomplished under the auspices of a teacher and, at the same time, not every person can completely identify the two extremes of moral behaviour in order to demonstrate the moderate and balanced path. Allāh, Who is the Absolute Wise, introduced all the Prophets, especially the Noble Prophet ﷺ, as the 'teacher and trainer' of morals,

---

[1] Noble Qur'an, Sūrat Ibrāhīm (14), Verse 5
وَ لَقَدْ أَرْسَلْنا مُوسىٰ بِآياتِنا أَنْ أَخْرِجْ قَوْمَكَ مِنَ الظُّلُماتِ إِلَى النُّورِ

[2] Ibid, Sūratul Ḥadīd (57), Verse 25
لَقَدْ أَرْسَلْنا رُسُلَنا بِالْبَيِّناتِ وَ أَنْزَلْنا مَعَهُمُ الْكِتابَ وَ الْمِيزانَ لِيَقُومَ النَّاسُ بِالْقِسْطِ

[3] Safīnatul Biḥār, Volume 1, Page 411. بُعِثْتُ لِأُتَمِّمَ مَكَارِمَ الْأَخْلَاقِ

so that the people, by following in his footsteps, distance themselves from vices and acquire the honour of the two worlds.

In the Qur'an, there exists a chapter by the name of القصص (The Narratives), which itself is proof that man is in need of stories and narratives.

In many places in the Qur'an, stories of Prophets, kings and nations have been mentioned. In addition, Allāh has presented issues pertaining to wars, peace, family, religion, society and other similar topics, in the form of stories and narratives. By reading these accounts, the people can comprehend and distinguish the paths of progress and regress, and ascent and descent in every field, especially morals.

The entire chapter Yūsuf has been devoted to the story of Yūsuf, Ya'qūb, Zulaikha and the brothers. In the beginning of the Chapter, Allāh says: "We narrate to you (O' Prophet) the most excellent of the narratives by (means of) what We have revealed to you this Qur'an."[4]

While, in the concluding verse of this very chapter, He says: "Indeed (there) in the histories of theirs, is a lesson for men of understanding."[5]

Indeed, one of the distinguished feats of the Qur'an is this very story of Yūsuf ﷺ, which it refers to as the 'best of the narratives', and at the end of which, it says: "In these stories there is a lesson for those, who desire to take a moral and adopt the path of the Perfect Men."

In this regard, Amīrul Mo'minīn ﷺ, in Nahjul Balāgha says to his son Imām Ḥasan ﷺ: "Even though I have not reached the age, which those before me have, yet I have looked into their behaviour and

[4] Noble Qur'an, Sūrat Yūsuf (12), Verse 3
نَحْنُ نَقُصُّ عَلَيْكَ أَحْسَنَ الْقَصَصِ بِما أَوْحَيْنا إِلَيْكَ هذَا الْقُرْآنَ

[5] Ibid, Verse 111 لَقَدْ كانَ فِي قَصَصِهِمْ عِبْرَةٌ لِأُولِي الْأَلْبابِ

reflected over the events of their lives. I walked amongst their ruins till I was as one of them. In fact, by virtue of those of their affairs that have become known to me, it is as though I have lived with them from the first to the last. I have therefore been able to discern the impure from the clean and the benefit from the harm. I have selected for you the choicest of those matters and collected for you their good points while keeping away from you the useless ones."

Years ago, I had written a book on ethics (for the treatment of vices), by the name of Ihyāul Qulūb. Ever since, I had been reflecting over the idea of compiling a book on moral stories. It so happened that, divinely, an opportunity came up before me and with it the motivation for undertaking this assignment. In spite of the lack of necessary books, I contented myself with those that were available and commenced the compilation of this book, recording four to five stories for every topic.

I have certainly not come across any book which has been compiled in this fashion. Books like Namunah-e-Ma'arif-e-Islam and Pand-e-Tārīkh have been present for around 30 years and I have made use of them too (in the course of this collection), but in those books, Qur'anic verses, traditions, poems and analogies have all been accumulated together; whereas, I have sought to satisfy myself by mentioning only the stories, while abstaining from presenting considerations relating to Qur'anic verses, traditions, poems and analogies, which would not only have increased the size of the book but would also have made it difficult to understand for many of the readers. This collection caters for the general public, young and old alike, who are acquainted with basic reading and writing. As far as possible, I have endeavoured to omit scientific issues and those aspects, pertaining to traditions, whose comprehension would be demanding and exacting for the general masses.

Although some of the stories may not possibly possess any aspect of reality and actuality, what I have focused on is the admonition and 'taking-a-lesson' aspect contained in them, which hopefully, the honourable readers would perceive and comprehend.

As far as the issue of associating a story to a particular topic is concerned, I do not claim that the stories allude to just one topic or that particular one which has been specified here; rather, there are stories which can be associated with several other topics too, in addition to the topic under which it has been mentioned here.

When narrating a text or presenting a translation, I have not restricted myself to the literal meaning but, for a better comprehension, have resorted to paraphrasing, allusion and conceptual explanation too.

To avoid interference of topics with one another and prolongation of discussion, I have refrained from bringing forth topics which are related to those already presented. For example, Ithār (altruism) has been presented as one of the topics but Infāq (spending in the path of Allāh) has been excluded.

To prevent the reader from experiencing exhaustion and boredom, and for the sake of variety, I have desisted from presenting stories of a monotonous kind, like those of philosophers and poets, but have strived to make the collection varied. In this way, the readers will, hopefully, derive a greater pleasure from the narratives.

In view of the fact that trustworthiness ought to be adhered to, I have referred every narrative presented here, to the book from which it has been extracted, also mentioning the volume and page. It is only with the objective of achieving a greater fluency of work that I have endeavoured to correct, polish or alter some of the words or sentences of the original text.

It is hoped that the readers, after going through the stories and narratives, reflect upon and take lessons from them so that they are able to create within themselves, a new impetus towards perfection of morals; and Allāh Willing, those who are endowed with laudable morals, should relate them to others, for rectification and remedy of the weaker souls.

Sayyid Ali Akbar Sadāqat

And our final prayer (is):
All Praise is due to Allāh, the Lord of the Worlds.

Mordad, 1378 [July 1999]

21 – Piety (Taqwa)

Allāh, the Wise, has said:

﴿ فَإِنَّ خَيْرَ الزَّادِ التَّقْوَى وَ اتَّقُوْنِ يَـــا أُولِي الأَلْبَابِ ﴾

"But the best of provisions is right conduct. So fear Me, O' ye that are wise."[6]

Imām ʿAlī عليه السلام said:

لاَ يُقَلُّ عَمَلٌ مَعَ تَقْوىً.

"No deed, if accompanied by piety, is trivial."[7]

Short Explanation:

Special taqwa is acquired by refraining from prohibited and dubious things, whereas *general* taqwa is acquired out of fear of punishment and the fire of Hell.

Taqwa is similar to the water of a river that flows by the trees growing along its banks, each tree benefiting from it in the measure of its tenderness, covetousness and essence. Although people benefit from piety according to their knowledge, perception and level of faith, their levels of piety differ in deeds and sincerity. In reality, piety is absolute obedience without any transgression, and (it is) knowledge without any ignorance. It becomes the cause for the acceptance of one's (good) deeds and makes one, who comes to possess it, distinguished and pre-eminent.[8]

---

[6] Noble Qur'an, Sūratul Baqarah (2), Verse 197

[7] Al-Kāfī , Volume 2, Page 61

[8] Tadhkeratul Ḥaqāiq, Page 79

1 – The Incorrect Piety

Once, during the era of the Noble Prophet ﷺ, three ladies approached him to complain about their husbands.

The first lady complained: "My husband has stopped eating meat."

"My husband has abandoned the use of perfume," the second one protested.

The third lady complained that her husband did not have intimate relations with her.

(By behaving in this manner, the husbands had desired to practice piety and abstinence).

This disturbed the Noble Prophet ﷺ so much that as he came out of his house, he did not even put on his cloak properly and thus, it dragged along the ground behind him.

Climbing the pulpit before a gathering of the people, he praised Allāh, and said: "Why is it that some of my companions do not eat meat, they do not apply perfume and they do not have intimate relations with their wives? O' Muslims! Do know that I too eat meat, make use of perfume and am intimate with my wives. This is my tradition and one who distances himself from my tradition is not from me."

In this manner, the Noble Prophet ﷺ destroyed the foundations of incorrect piety and condemned its advocates.[9]

2 – Abū Dharr

Abū Dharr said: "My provisions and savings during the time of the Noble Prophet ﷺ had always been three kilograms of dates. As long as I live, I shall never seek to possess more than this quantity."

---

[9] Hikāyat-hā-e-Shanīdani, Volume 2, Page 74; Al-Kāfī, Volume 5, Page 496

ʿAtā says: I noticed Abū Dharr offering prayers in an old garment. "O' Abū Dharr! Don't you have a better garment?" I asked him.

"If I had one, you would have seen me in it," he replied.

"But for a period, I had seen you with two outfits," I said.

"I gave the other one to my nephew, who was in greater need than me."

"By Allāh! You are needy yourself," I exclaimed.

He raised his head towards the sky and implored, "Indeed! O' Lord! I am in need of Your forgiveness."

He then turned to me and continued, "It appears that you have come to regard this world as something very important and significant. In addition to this garment that you presently see on me, I have one more garment which is exclusive for the mosque, some goats which provide me with milk, some food, a wooden case in which I carry my belongings and a wife who relieves me from the troubles of cooking; what bounty could be greater than what I possess?"

◈◈◈

Some people suggested to Abū Dharr, "Do you not desire to purchase properties for yourself as the others have done for themselves?"

"What need do I have to become an aristocrat or a nobleman?" he replied. "A drink of milk and water every day and a (small) amount of wheat in a week are quite sufficient for me!"[10]

3 – A Drunkard is not to be Trusted

Ismāʾīl, the eldest son of Imām Ṣādiq ﷺ, had some money in his possession. When he learned that a person from the tribe of Quraish who was living in Madinah, was about to set out for Yemen, he decided

[10] Paighambar Wa Yārān, Volume 1, Page 47; Aʿyān al-Shīʿa, Page 329 – 347

to hand him some money so that he could purchase for him some merchandise for trade.

When Ismā'īl consulted his father, Imām Ṣādiq عليه السلام about the issue, the Imām عليه السلام inquired: "Does the man consume intoxicants?"

"People say so, but how do we know they speak the truth?" replied Ismā'īl.

The Imām عليه السلام advised him, "It is not in your interest to give him the money."

But Ismā'īl still gave his money to the person, who proceeded on his trip and in the course of it, embezzled the funds.

During the season of Ḥajj, both Imām Ṣādiq عليه السلام and Ismā'īl went on pilgrimage. Ismā'īl was in the process of performing the Tawaf of the Ka'bah when the Imām عليه السلام noticed that he was continually beseeching Allāh to redeem his losses.

Manoeuvring himself through the crowd, the Imām عليه السلام reached his son and placing his hand upon his shoulder, squeezed it lightly and said: "My Son! Do not seek anything from Allāh needlessly, for you have no right upon Him. You should not have trusted the person in the first place. It is not upon others to rectify one's own wrongdoing."

"The people used to say that he consumed intoxicants but I had not seen him consume it!" said Ismā'īl.

The Imām عليه السلام advised him further: "Consider the talks of the believers to be correct and do not trust a drunkard; be wary of giving money to those who are foolish and weak of understanding just as has been stated in the Qur'an[11]. Who could be more foolish than a drunkard? Suggestions and intermediation of a drunkard in issues related to marriage should not be accepted nor should one place trust in his

[11] Noble Qur'an, Sūratul Nisā (5), Verse 5 (لَا تُؤْتُوا السُّفَهَاءَ أَمْوَالَكُمُ الَّتِي جَعَلَ اللهُ لَكُمْ قِيَاماً)

possession for he is bound to misappropriate it. A person who relies on a drunkard has no right whatsoever upon Allāh that he may seek from Him compensation for damages suffered by him."[12]

4 - Sheikh Murtadha Anṣārī

The late Sheikh Murtadha Anṣārī, in the company of his brother, travelled from Kāshān to Mashhad and then arrived in Tehran where he eventually settled down in Mādershah madrasah in which he shared a room with one of the students.

One day, the Sheikh gave the student some money so that he could buy some bread for both of them. When the student returned, the Sheikh noticed that he had brought some sweetmeat too, which he had placed on top of the bread. Turning to the student, he said: "From where did you get the money to purchase the sweetmeat?"

"I borrowed it," replied the student.

The Sheikh took only that portion of the bread that had no sweetmeat on it, saying: "I shall not eat the sweetmeat for I am not sure I may live long enough to repay the debt!"

Years later, when that student came to Najaf, he went to the Sheikh and asked: "Now that you are at the head of the Ḥawza ʿIlmiyyah and the Marjaʿ of the entire Shīʿa world, tell me, what did you do that Allāh granted you this great success?"

"It is because I did not have the courage to eat even that portion of the bread which lay beneath the sweetmeat, but you had the audacity to eat the bread as well as the sweetmeat!" replied the Sheikh.[13]

---

[12] Bā Mardum In Guneh Barkhord Konīm, Page 35; Biḥārul Anwār, Volume 4, Page 267

[13] Dāstān-hā Wa Pand-hā, Volume 4, Page 151; Zindagi Wa Shakhsiyyat-e-Sheikh Anṣārī, Page 70

5 – The Objection of ʿAqīl

Once, after becoming the caliph, Imām ʿAlī عليه السلام ascended the pulpit, praised Allāh and said to the assembly: "By Allāh, as long as I have in my possession (even) one branch of a date-palm, I shall not extend my hand towards your wealth. I am depriving myself of this wealth and am giving it to you."

At this point ʿAqīl, the brother of Imām عليه السلام, stood up. "By Allāh! You have placed me on par with that black person from Madinah," he said.

"Sit down! There is none except you, who could have spoken out in this gathering. You do not possess any kind of superiority over that black person, save for precedence in Islam, piety and reward, and these are issues which bring about superiority in the Hereafter," Imām ʿAlī عليه السلام cautioned him.[14]

[14] Namunah-e-Maʿarif, Volume 3, Page 171; Al-Wāfī, Volume 3, Page 60

22 – Trust In Allāh

Allāh, the Wise, has said:

﴿ فَإِذَا عَزَمْتَ فَتَوَكَّلْ عَلَى اللَّهِ إِنَّ اللَّهَ يُحِبُّ الْمُتَوَكِّلِينَ ﴾

"So when you have decided, then place your trust in Allāh; surely Allāh loves those who trust."[15]

Imām ʿAlī ﷺ said:

أَلتَّوَكُّلُ عَلَى اللهِ نَجَاةٌ مِنْ كُلِّ سُوْءٍ.

"Placing one's trust in Allāh is the means of deliverance from every evil."[16]

Short Explanation

Tawakkul (placing one's trust in Allāh) is a jar that has been sealed with Allāh's seal, and only that person who does not rely on Allāh and place his trust in Him, shall break open the seal of the jar and consume its contents.

The lowest grade of tawakkul is when a person does not strive to act upon his own principles before the right time, and does not endeavour to acquire more than what has been ordained for him. The essence of tawakkul is entrusting one's affairs to Allāh, and if a person is heedless towards the actual 'cause', i.e. Allāh, he shall not achieve the reality of tawakkul.

Tawakkul can never be realized by mere words and claims, rather, it is an internal and esoteric issue, which finds its roots in faith and belief,

[15] Noble Qur'an, Surat Āle ʿImrān (3), Verse 159
[16] Biḥārul Anwār, Volume 78, Page 79

and it is by abandoning all hopes and aspirations that a person can arrive at the reality of tawakkul.[17]

1 – The Trader who Placed his Trust in Allāh

During the time of the Noble Prophet ﷺ there lived a trader who, in all affairs, always placed his trust in Allāh. He used to travel from Syria to Madinah for trade and during one of his trips, he was confronted by a bandit who drew his sword and intended to kill him.

"If it is my wealth that you desire, come and take it and leave me alone," pleaded the trader.

"Killing you is a must, for if I let you go free, you will identify me to the authorities," said the bandit.

"In that case give me respite till I have offered a two rak'at prayer," requested the trader.

The bandit agreed and the trader engaged himself in prayers. Having completed the prayers, he raised his hands and beseeched: 'O' Lord! I have heard from Your Prophet that whoever places his trust in You shall remain protected. I have no helper in this desert and Your grace is my only hope.'

Having placed all his trust in Allāh, he had hardly completed his supplication when a rider on a white horse loomed in the distance. When he came close, the rider confronted the bandit and killed him with one stroke of his sword. Then, turning to the trader, he said: "O' You, who places your trust in Allāh! I have killed the enemy of Allāh and He has delivered you from him."

"Who are you that you have come to my assistance in this desert?" the trader asked.

---

[17] Tadhkerah al-Ḥaqāiq, Page 72

"I am your *tawakkul.* Allāh brought me out in the form of an Angel and I was in the heavens when Jibra'īl called out to me and said: "Hasten to the assistance of your master and exterminate his enemy", and here I have come and eliminated your enemy." Having said thus, he disappeared out of sight.

The trader fell down in prostration of thanksgiving to Allāh and acquired a stronger conviction with respect to the instructions of the Noble Prophet ﷺ regarding tawakkul. On arrival in Madinah, he approached the Noble Prophet ﷺ and narrated what had transpired.

"Indeed! Tawakkul raises a person to the pinnacle of success and the rank of a person who possesses it, is equivalent to the ranks of the Prophets, the friends of Allāh, the righteous ones and the martyrs," said the Prophet ﷺ.[18]

2 - The Noble Prophet and Trust in Allāh

When Abū Sufiyān, the chief of the polytheists of Makkah, saw the ten thousand strong army of Islam (during the conquest of Makkah), he was filled with awe and astonishment. As he walked beside the battalions of the Noble Prophet ﷺ, he murmured: "I wish I knew why Muḥammad became victorious over me. How did he manage to gather for himself such a powerful army despite being alone and without support in Makkah?"

The Noble Prophet ﷺ overheard him. "We became victorious over you by Allāh's assistance!" he said, placing his hand upon Abū Sufiyān's shoulder.

In the battle of Ḥunain, when the enemy suddenly and unsuspectingly attacked the forces of Islam, chaos reigned supreme within the Muslim ranks. When the Noble Prophet ﷺ watched this state of the Muslim army, he sought Allāh's help by placing his trust in Him, and

[18] Khazīnatul Jawāhir, Page 679; Majālis al-Muttaqīn (of Shahīd-e-Thālith)

supplicated: '*O' Lord! All praise and thanks only belong to You. I place my complaint (regarding the state of affairs) before You and it is only You from whom help and assistance ought to be sought.*'

At that moment, Jibra'īl descended from the heavens and said to him: "O' Prophet of Allāh! You have recited a supplication which Mūsā عليه السلام had recited when the sea had split for him and he was granted deliverance from the evils of Fir'awn."[19]

3 - The Illness of Prophet Mūsā

Once, Prophet Mūsā عليه السلام became ill. The Banī Israel came to him and realizing what his illness was, advised him: "If you consume such and such medicine you will recover from your sickness."

"I shall not seek any cure but will instead wait till Allāh cures me without the help of any medicine," said Mūsā عليه السلام to them. His illness became prolonged whereupon Allāh revealed to him: "By My Majesty and Glory! I shall never cure you till you have consumed the medicine which they had recommended to you."

Mūsā عليه السلام asked the Banī Israel to treat him with the medicine that they had previously suggested. They treated him and shortly after that, Mūsā عليه السلام regained his health. However, this incident left Mūsā عليه السلام with a feeling of complaint and dejection but Allāh revealed to him: "You desired to annul My Wisdom by means of your trust in Me! Is there one, other than Me, who has placed the medicinal and beneficial effects in plants and various things?" [20]

---

[19] Dars-hāi Az Zindagi-e-Payāmbar-e-Islam, Page 216; Biḥārul Anwār, Volume 21, Page 150

[20] Jāme' al-Sa'ādāt, Volume 3, Page 228; 'Ilm-e-Akhlāq-e-Islāmī, Volume 2, Page 290

4 - Ḥammād Ibn Ḥabīb

Ḥammād Ibn Ḥabīb Kūfī narrates: "One year, I had set out for Ḥajj accompanied by some people. Just as we passed by a place called Zubālah, a dreadful wind with black dust began to blow. Its intensity was so great and severe that everyone in the group were left scattered. I found myself alone and lost in a place with no water or trees. It was not long before night fell. Staring into the distance, my eyes perceived the silhouette of a single tree and I began trudging towards it. As I approached the tree, I witnessed that a youth, dressed in white apparel and scented with musk, also came up to the tree.

'This person must be one of the auliya of Allāh!' I thought.

I concealed myself fearing that if I came forward, he would move away to another place. The youth readied himself for his prayers, recited:

يَا مَنْ حَاذَ كُلَّ شَيْءٍ مَلَكُوْتاً

and then started his prayers.

I noticed that there was a spring of water nearby. I performed my ablution and stood behind the youth for my prayers. I observed that in the course of his prayers, when the youth reached the verses that narrated Divine chastisement and punishment, he would repeat them with wailing, weeping and lamentation. After the prayers, the youth began to walk away from his place, all the while supplicating:

يَا مَنْ قَصَدَهُ الضَّالُّونَ

Fearing that I might lose him, I rushed toward him and pleaded: "I place you under the oath of He Who has taken away exhaustion from you and instilled within you the ecstasy of this solitude! Have pity upon me for I have lost my way and I (also) desire to be adorned with your traits and attributes."

"If you had truly placed your trust in Allāh, you would never have lost your way. Now follow me," replied the youth.

Saying this, he went to one side of the tree and, taking hold of my hand, brought me to a place by means of tayy al-ardh[21]. It became apparent to me that morning had dawned.

"Good news for you, for this place is Makkah," said the youth.

I realized that I could hear the voices of the pilgrims who had come there to perform the Ḥajj. I turned to the youth and asked: "I place you under the oath of He, upon Whom you have pinned your hopes for the Day of Judgment! Tell me, who are you?"

"Since you have placed me under oath, I shall inform you of my identity. I am ʿAlī Ibn Ḥusain (Zainul ʿĀbidīn)," the youth answered.'"[22]

5 – Relying upon the Butler

Jibraʾīl came to Prophet Yūsuf ﷺ while he was in prison and asked him: "O' Yūsuf! Who made you the most beautiful of all men?"

Yūsuf replied, "Allāh."

Jibraʾīl questioned again, "Who made you the most beloved of all children in the eyes of your father?"

"My Allāh," said Yūsuf.

"Who directed the caravan towards the well (into which you were thrown)?"

"My Lord," replied Yūsuf.

"Who protected you from the stone which the people of the caravan had hurled into the well?"

---

[21] Literally: *Folding up of the earth.* Covering a great distance in a fraction of a moment, miraculously. (Tr.)

[22] Pand-e-Tārīkh, Volume 5, Page 182; Biḥārul Anwār, Volume 11, Page 24

"Allāh."

"Who delivered you from the well?"

"My Allāh."

"Who protected you from the deceit of the ladies?"

"My Lord."

Jibra'īl finally concluded, "Allāh says: What made you seek your need from someone other than Me? For this act, you shall stay in prison for seven years (for the offense of placing your trust in the king's barman and asking him to seek your freedom from the king)."

◈◈◈

According to another tradition, Allāh revealed to him: "O' Yūsuf! Who was it who showed you that dream?"

Yūsuf replied, "It was You, O' My Lord!"

"Who protected you from the guiles of the wife of the King of Egypt?" asked Allāh.

"It was You, O' My Lord!"

Allāh declared, "(Then) why did you seek help from someone else and not from Me? Had you placed your trust in Me, I would have liberated you from your imprisonment, but now that you have placed your trust in someone else, you must stay in prison for seven years."

(After this) Yūsuf wept so much in prison that his inmates became frustrated with him and it was decided that he would only weep on alternate days.[23]

[23] Namunah-e-Ma'arif, Volume 3, Page 280; Layālīul Akhbār, Page 92

23 – Submission

Allāh, the Wise, has said:

﴿ وَ أُمِرْنَا لِنُسْلِمَ لِرَبِّ الْعَالَمِينَ ﴾

"And we are commanded that we should submit to the Lord of the worlds."[24]

Imām Bāqir ﷺ said:

أَحَقُّ خَلْقِ اللّٰهِ أَنْ يُسْلِمَ لِمَا قَضَى اللّٰهُ.

"The most worthy of Allāh's servants is one who submits before divine decree."[25]

Short Explanation

The attribute of taslīm[26] holds a rank higher than those of ridhā[27] and tawakkul[28]. This is because a person who possesses this attribute abandons his own quest for seeking solutions to the problems that plague him and instead, dissociates himself from his inner attachments to such an extent that he hands himself over to Allāh completely.

In the attribute of Riḍā, the actions are generally consistent with human inclination and temperament, while in tawakkul, people take Allāh as their agent, but such is not the case in the attribute of tasleem. The chosen ones of Allāh are afflicted with various kinds of difficulties such as an ill-tempered spouse, poverty, disease, harassment by the people, and so on; but having submitted themselves

---

[24] Noble Qur'an, Sūratul An'ām (6), Verse 71
[25] Jāme' al-Sa'adāt, Volume 3, Page 204
[26] Submission to the will of Allāh. (Tr.)
[27] Satisfaction and pleasure over divine decree. (Tr.)
[28] Complete reliance upon Allāh. (Tr.)

totally, they neither voice any protest nor do they experience any sort of unhappiness over these afflictions.

1 – The Imām's Reply

It has been narrated that sometimes, Imām Ṣādiq عليه السلام entertained his guests with sweetmeat and porridge, whereas at other times, he presented them with olives and plain bread.

A person once said to him: "If you manage your affairs with prudence (and foresight), you will always be consistent and will thus be able to entertain your guests in the same manner at all times."

"The management of our affairs lies in Allāh's hands (and we are in total submission to His Will). Whenever He grants us (an increased livelihood), we cater for our guests and ourselves liberally but whenever He restrains our livelihood, we too adjust our lives accordingly," replied the Imām عليه السلام.[29]

2 – Mu'ādh Ibn Jabal

Mu'ādh embraced Islam at the age of eighteen and participated in the battles of Badr, Uhud, Khandaq and some others. The Noble Prophet صلى الله عليه وآله وسلم established the bond of brotherhood between him and 'Abdullāh Ibn Mas'ud.

Mu'ādh was compassionate by nature and possessed a pleasant personality. The Noble Prophet صلى الله عليه وآله وسلم sent him to Yemen as its governor and showered him with numerous advices, one of them being: "Do not be too strict with the people; behave with them in such a manner that they are attracted to your speech and religion."

During the Caliphate of the second Caliph, a battle ensued between the Muslims and the Romans and Mu'ādh participated in it too. In the year 18 AH, in 'Amwās, Syria, an epidemic of plague began to spread. Abū

[29] Shanīdani-hā-e-Tārīkh, Page 32; Maḥajjatul Baiḍā, Volume 3, Page 43

'Ubaidah, the commander of the Muslim army, was afflicted with the disease and when he realized that his death was inevitable, he appointed Muʿādh as his successor. The soldiers requested Muʿādh to pray for an end to the calamity but he declined to do so.

"This is not a calamity. Instead, it is a prayer of your Prophet ﷺ; death of the pious and righteous ones, and martyrdom, which Allāh grants to only a few from amongst you," he said.

He then supplicated: "O' Lord! Grant the household of Muʿādh their complete share of this Mercy (plague)."

Shortly afterwards, members of his household were afflicted with the disease and succumbed to it. When he too sensed its effects in his finger, he placed the finger in his mouth and biting it, said, "O' Lord! This is small and trivial; make it blessed (for me)."

He eventually died of this plague (in the year 18 AH) at the age of 38 and was buried near Jordan.[30]

3 – Learn Submission from the Pigeons

During the time of one of the prophets, there lived a lady who had a son who was in his youth and whom she loved dearly. As divine decree would have it, the son died leaving the mother greatly aggrieved and immensely disturbed. She was in such a state that her relatives approached the prophet of the time and sought his help.

When he came to the mother, the prophet found her in a state of sorrow and agitation and was weeping. His eyes then fell upon a pigeon-nest nearby. He turned to the lady and asked: "O' Lady! Is this a pigeon-nest?"

The lady replied that it was.

---

[30] Paighambar Wa Yārān, Pages 264–259; Tabaqāt Ibn Saʿd, Volume 3, Pages 122-124

"Do the pigeons give birth to their young ones?" asked the prophet.

"Yes."

"Do all the young ones grow up to be able to fly?"

"No, we kill some of them for their flesh," said the lady.

The prophet continued, "And despite this, these pigeons do not abandon their nest?"

"No, they do not move away to another place," replied the lady.

The prophet then advised, "O' Lady! Be apprehensive lest you be worse off than these pigeons in the eyes of your Lord. These pigeons, despite the fact that you kill and eat their young ones in front of their eyes, do not turn away from you. Whereas you, as a result of losing just one son, have directed your anger towards Allāh, turned away from Him, exhibited all this agitation, and uttered things that are inappropriate."

Hearing these words, her tears ceased and she never displayed impatience and discontent thenceforth.[31]

4 – Sa'sah

Ahnaf Ibn Qais narrates: "Once, I complained to my paternal uncle Sa'sah, of stomach ache. Instead of sympathising with me, he rebuked me severely by saying: "O' Nephew! Whenever you experience any discomfort and you complain about it to another being similar to yourself, there can exist only two possibilities on the issue: the person to whom you have narrated your problem is either your friend, in which case, quite obviously, he too would be concerned for you; or he is your enemy, in which case he would be delighted over your disturbed state.

[31] Namunah-e-Ma'ārif, Volume 2, Page 761

Do not manifest your problem to someone who is like you and does not possess the power to free you from it; instead seek shelter in, and present the problem to Him, Who has afflicted you with it, for it is He, Who can rid you of it.

O' Nephew! It has been forty years since one of my eyes lost its vision but I have not revealed this to anyone - not even my wife knows that I am blind in one eye!"[32]

5 – Submission before a Ruling

The date-plantation of Zubaīr Ibn ʿAwwām (a cousin of the Noble Prophet ﷺ) lay adjacent to that of one of the Anṣār (the Helpers). Once, there arose a dispute between them in respect of the irrigation of their lands.

In order to resolve the dispute they approached the Noble Prophet ﷺ and presented the problem to him. Taking into account the fact that the plantation of Zubaīr lay near the upper part of the land where the water came from, while that of the other person was near the lower section (and it was the customary practice that the upper part would be watered before the lower one), the Noble Prophet ﷺ ruled that it should be Zubaīr, who should water his plantation first, followed by the person from the Anṣār.

Despite the totally just nature of the ruling, the Anṣār was displeased and protested to the Noble Prophet ﷺ saying: "You have ruled in Zubaīr's favour as he happens to be your cousin."

The Noble Prophet ﷺ was so greatly upset at this antagonistic staement that the colour of his face changed. At this juncture, the following verse was revealed: "*But no! By your Lord! They do not believe (in reality) until they make you a judge of that which has become a matter of disagreement among them, and then do not find*

[32] Pand-e-Tārīkh, Volume 5, Page 188; Al-Kunā Wa al-Alqāb, Volume 2, Page 13

any straitness in their hearts as to what you have decided and submit with entire submission.'[33]

This verse indicates that nobody can express dissatisfaction with the ruling of the leader of an Islamic government of the Noble Prophet ﷺ and seek to follow his own inclinations. One should submit totally to the verdict given.[34]

[33] Noble Qur'an, Sūratul Nisā (4), Verse 65 (و يُسَلِّمُوا تَسلِيمًا)

[34] Dāstān-hā Wa Pand-hā, Volume 9, Page 102; Majma'ul Bayān, Volume 3, Page 69

24 – Contemplation

Allāh, the Wise, has said:

﴿ اَوَلَمْ يَتَفَكَّرُوا فِي أَنْفُسِهِمْ مَا خَلَقَ اللّٰهُ السَّمٰوَاتِ وَ الأَرْضَ وَ مَا بَيْنَهُمَا إِلاَّ بِالْحَقِّ وَ أَجَلٍ مُسَمًّى ﴾

"Do they not reflect within themselves: Allāh did not create the heavens and the earth and what is between them two but with truth, and (for) an appointed term?" [35]

Imām ʿAlī ﷷ said:

أَلتَّفَكُّرُ يَدْعُو إِلَى الْبِرِّ وَ الْعَمَلِ بِهِ.

"Contemplation invites (man) towards good (deed) and its performance." [36]

Short Explanation

Reflecting over one's own state and that of the other people leads to the manifestation of the good, expiation of sins and illumination of the heart. It draws a person's attention towards his Hereafter and brings about an increase in his or her (good) deeds.

Contemplation is a quality and an act of worship, the like of which there is none - just as the Noble Prophet ﷺ has said: "An hour of contemplation is superior to an entire year's worship." Only he, upon whose heart Allāh has cast His glance and illuminated it with the light of His cognizance, can reach the station of contemplation, whereupon he then begins to perceive the world with a vision of comprehension and understanding, and never becomes heedless of Allāh.[37]

---

[35] Noble Qur'an, Sūratul Rūm (30), Verse 8
[36] Jāmeʿ al-Saʿadāt, Volume 1, Page 166
[37] Tadhkerah al-Ḥaqāiq, Page 29

1 – Rabiʿah

Rabiʿah Ibn Kaʿb reports: "Once, the Noble Prophet ﷺ said to me: "O' Rabiʿah! You have been serving me for seven years and therefore, will you not ask for something from me in order that I grant it to you?"

"O' Prophet of Allāh! Grant me some time in order that I may reflect over the matter," I requested. The next day, when I had arrived in his presence, the Prophet ﷺ said: "O' Rabi'ah! Speak out your wish."

"Pray to Allāh that He makes me enter Paradise along with you!" I said.

Hearing this request, he inquired, "Who is it that has taught you to seek this from me?"

"No one has taught it to me. I considered that if I sought great wealth, it would eventually get exhausted; if I sought a long life and numerous children, the ultimate eventuality would be death; hence, as a result of this contemplation, I eventually opted for this request," I replied.

The Noble Prophet ﷺ lowered his head for a few moments as he deliberated, after which, raising his head, he said: "I shall seek your wish from Allāh, but you must help me too (in this matter) by prostrating excessively."[38]

2 – Contemplation before Action

One of the companions of the Noble Prophet ﷺ said to him: "I always tend to suffer losses in my business transactions. The guile and deception of the sellers or the purchasers act like magic and leave me cheated."

The Noble Prophet ﷺ advised: "In every transaction in which you fear that you might be deceived, demand from the person with whom you are doing business with the right to annul the transaction within a

[38] Khazīnatul Jawāhir, Page 345; Al-Daʿwāt (By Rāwandī)

period of three days. This is for the reason that should you happen to suffer losses, you would be able to take back your money. In addition, be patient and forbearing in the course of the transaction.

"Do know that contemplation and patience are from Allāh, while hastiness and impetuosity are from Shaitān. You can learn this lesson from a dog, for when you throw a piece of bread to a dog, it does not immediately begin to eat it but first smells it and after finding it to be appropriate, begins eating it; similarly, you should smell every matter that comes up before you (i.e. reflect and ponder over the pros and cons of it and do not embark upon it without the preliminaries). You, with your intellect and wisdom, are no less than a dog; thus, contemplate and reflect before every action."[39]

3 – Types of Contemplation

Miqdād, one of the loyal companions of ʿAlī ﷺ, says: "I went to Abū Huraīrah who said that he had heard the Noble Prophet ﷺ say: 'Contemplating for an hour is better than the worship of one year.'

I went to Ibn ʿAbbās and heard him say that the Noble Prophet ﷺ said: 'Contemplation for one hour is superior to seven years of worship.'

I went to another companion and heard him narrate that the Noble Prophet ﷺ said: 'An hour of contemplation is better than seventy years of worship.'

I was astonished to hear each of them narrating differently from the other and so, I approached the Noble Prophet ﷺ and informed him of the three different versions. He said: "All three of them speak the truth." Then, in order to prove his point, he summoned the three men. All of us gathered in the presence of the Noble Prophet ﷺ.

[39] Riwāyat-hā Wa Hikāyat-hā, Page 195; Dāstān-hā-e-Mathnawī, Volume 2, Page 125

The Noble Prophet ﷺ asked Abū Hurairah: "How do you contemplate?"

"As stated by Allāh in the Qur'an: '*(Men of understanding) reflect on the creation of the heavens and the earth.*'[40]. I too reflect upon the wonders of the heavens and the earth," he replied.

The Noble Prophet ﷺ remarked, "One hour of your contemplation is better than one year of worship."

Then turning to Ibn ʿAbbās, he asked, "How do you contemplate?"

"I reflect upon death and the horrors of the Day of Judgment," replied Ibn ʿAbbās.

The Noble Prophet ﷺ said, "One hour of your contemplation is better than seven years of worship." Then, he asked the other companion, "In what manner do you contemplate?"

The companion answered, "I reflect upon the fire of Hell and its dreadfulness and severity."

"One hour of your contemplation is better than seventy years of worship," the Noble Prophet ﷺ stated.

In this way the issue was solved and it became clear that the rewards for contemplation depended upon the intention that accompanied it.[41]

4 – Thoughts of Leadership

Saʿdi narrates: "One of my friends who was disturbed and distressed due to his meagre livelihood, complained to me about his low income and a large family."

"In order to safeguard my reputation, I intend to shift to another city so that no one becomes aware of the abject state of my affairs," he

[40] Noble Qur'an, Sūrat Āle ʿImrān (3), Verse 191

[41] Dastān-hā Wa Pand-hā, Volume 5, Page 87; Tafsīr Rūḥul Bayān, Volume 8, Page 440

said. “You are aware that I know accounting and can maintain accounts; I have approached you so that you use your rank and position to get me a job in the government so that I might lead my remaining life with peace of mind and will be grateful to you for your efforts!”

I said to him, “Handling the accounts of the king entails two aspects; on the one hand it carries hope while on the other hand it is also work which has to be feared. Do not place yourself in an ominous situation for the hope which the work possesses.”

“In view of my condition, your advice appears to be inappropriate; in addition, you have not responded correctly to my request,” said the friend.

“You surely possess piety, knowledge and trustworthiness but (do realize that) envious and fault-finding individuals lie in wait for you. It is in your own interest that you lead your life with contentment and abandon the idea of a high rank and post,” I explained.

My friend was upset when he heard this and said, “What kind of reasoning and deliberation is this? It is in times of need that friends should step forward for help, for in good times even enemies pretend to be one’s friend.”

Sensing his embarrassment over my advice, I took him to the minister of treasury who was known to me. I narrated to him my friend’s plight and the minister assigned him the responsibility of a petty task.

As time passed, the officials found him to be vigilant and pleasant-mannered and so promoted him. After a long time, I embarked on a journey to Makkah with some of my friends. On the way back, not far from my city, I came across my friend who seemed to be in a state of distress. He came towards me looking depressed.

“Why are you in such a state?” I asked him.

"Just as you had predicted, a group of people became envious of me and accused me of treason," he responded. "The king, without any investigation, threw me into prison and subjected me to torture and punishment. I remained in prison till the news of the return of the pilgrims reached the city, whereupon I was set free. The king even went to the extent of confiscating the inheritance which I had received from my father."

Ṣaʿdī continues: "I said to him, 'I had advised you previously that working for kings is similar to a journey by sea – beneficial, but at the same time, dangerous – you might either strike treasure or end up in destruction, but you refused to take heed!'"[42]

5 – The Kingdom of Rey or Killing the Imām

Yazīd instructed his governor, ʿUbaidullāh Ibn Ziyād, that if Ḥusain ﷺ refused to pledge allegiance, he should fight the Imām ﷺ.

Prior to the incident of Kerbala, ʿUbaidullāh Ibn Ziyād had appointed ʿUmar Ibn Saʿd as governor of the province of Rey, but before he could go there, ʿUbaidullāh Ibn Ziyād sent him a letter, which contained the following instructions: 'Ḥusain ﷺ has arrived in Iraq. First proceed to Iraq, fight with him, kill him and then proceed towards Rey.'

ʿUmar Ibn Saʿd approached ʿUbaidullāh and requested: "O' Amir! Relieve me of this responsibility!"

"I shall relieve you of this responsibility but I shall also relieve you of the governorship of Rey," ʿUbaidullāh responded.

ʿUmar Ibn Saʿd found himself hesitating between fighting the Imām ﷺ and governing the great kingdom of Rey. He requested ʿUbaidullāh to give him respite for a night so that he could reflect over the matter. ʿUbaidullāh agreed and ʿUmar Ibn Saʿd passed the entire night

---

[42] Hikāyat-hā-e-Gulistān, Page 65

pondering over the matter till he eventually opted for the kingdom of Rey, which lay before him at that moment, but chose to disregard Hell and Paradise, which were in the next life. He decided to fight the Imām عليه السلام.

The next morning, he went to ʿUbaidullāh and expressed his readiness to accept the responsibility of fighting the Imām عليه السلام. ʿUbaidullāh placed a huge army at his disposal so that he could proceed to Kerbala for the purpose.

Imām Ḥusain عليه السلام entered Kerbala on the 2nd of Muḥarram while ʿUmar Ibn Saʿd, in his capacity as the supreme commander of his army and with a four thousand strong cavalry, arrived there on the 3rd.

He appointed Shimr as the chief of his army and on the 10th of Muḥarram went to the extent of ordering the killing of Imām Ḥusain عليه السلام and seventy two of his children and companions just for the purpose of acquiring the kingdom of Rey."[43]

[43] Muntahal Aʿmāl, Volume 1, Page 333

25 – Humiliation

Allāh, the Wise, has said:

﴿ يَا أَيُّهَا الَّذِينَ آمَنُوا لاَ يَسْخَرْ قَوْمٌ مِنْ قَوْمٍ ﴾

"O you who believe! let not (one) people laugh at (another) people."[44]

The Noble Prophet ﷺ said:

مَنْ حَقَرَ مُؤْمِناً مِسْكِيناً أَوْ غَيْرَ مِسْكِينٍ لَمْ يَزَلِ اللّٰهُ عَزَّ وَ جَلَّ حَاقِراً لَهُ مَاقِتاً.

"If a person humiliates a believer, indigent or otherwise, Allāh shall always abhor and humiliate him."[45]

Short Explanation

Factors such as arrogance, malice, envy and the like cause some individuals to view others who are either illiterate or lack strength and whom they have compelled into performing base and lowly work, with contempt and humiliation.

Disparagement in every form is forbidden; moreover, if the humiliated person experiences a feeling of disgrace and injury, this is bound to result in a metaphysical reaction which would reflect badly upon the esteem and personality of the offender. Thus, it is befitting to take regard of the weakest of Allāh's creations so that, we too are encompassed by His grace and compassion.

1 – Mufaḍḍhal Ibn ʿUmar

Once, a letter signed by some of the Shiite elders, was brought to Imām Ṣādiq عليه السلام by a few of the signatories themselves. The letter complained of the friendship of Mufaḍḍhal Ibn ʿUmar, the Imām's

[44] Noble Qur'an, Sūratul Ḥujarāt (49), Verse 11
[45] Jāmeʿ al-Saʿadāt, Volume 2, Page 215

representative in Kufah, with some pigeon-fanciers, who were apparently not of good character.

After reading the letter, the Imām ﷺ wrote and sent a letter to Mufaḍḍhal through those very individuals who had brought the complaint to him.

Perchance, the Imām's letter reached Mufaḍḍhal while some of the signatories of the letter of complaint were present in his house.

Opening the letter in their presence, he read it and then handed it over to them. When the signatories read the letter, they found that it contained some instructions from Imām ﷺ to Mufaḍḍhal, requiring him to arrange a transaction involving a large amount of money. The letter did not make the slightest reference to Mufaḍḍhal's association with the pigion-fanciers.

Since the issue concerned the raising of money, Mufaḍḍhal's guests lowered their heads and said that they needed time to think about it. They asked to be excused from making any monetary contribution.

Mufaḍḍhal, the intelligent person that he was, requested them to stay over for food and prevented them from leaving his house. In the meantime, he sent word to the pigeon-fanciers asking them to come to his house. When they had arrived, he read out the Imām's letter to them in full view of the previous group. Without wasting any time, the pigeon-fanciers left and while the previous group was still engaged in consuming the food, they returned, handed over a large amount of money to Mufaḍḍhal and then took his leave.

At this point, Mufaḍḍhal turned to the complainants and said: "Despite the fact that these youths help the religion when the occasion demands and there exists a great possibility that they may turn to the right path, you desire that I should not entertain them and associate with them? Do you think Allāh is in need of your prayers and fasts that you have become so haughty over them, but when it comes to money, you seek excuses and refuse to answer the call of the Imām عليه السلام?"

The elders who had viewed Mufaḍḍhal's friendship with those youths with contempt, were left mortified and speechless as they departed from his house.[46]

2 - The Conduct of the Noble Prophet

The Noble Prophet ﷺ and a few other individuals were having their meal when a person, suffering from smallpox, came to the gathering. His disease was so acute that the boils had become septic. Every person, near whom this diseased person tried to sit, would show his revulsion and loathing by rising up and moving away from him. (Noticing this) the Noble Prophet ﷺ made the person sit beside himself and exhibited great kindness towards him.

◈◈◈

On another occasion, the Noble Prophet ﷺ, together with a few of his companions, was busy having his food when a leper arrived in the gathering. The people present expressed their abhorrence and detestation over his arrival but the Noble Prophet ﷺ asked him to sit next to himself and invited him to eat the food.

A person from the Quraish, who had displayed his aversion, was afflicted with the same disease before meeting his death![47]

3 - The Consequence of Holding Someone in Contempt

There lived amongst Banī Isrā'īl, a person who was so sinful and immoral that they eventually had him expelled from their midst.

---

[46] Ba Mardum In Guneh Barkhord Konīm, Page 78; Manhajul Maqāl of Astarābādi, Page 343

[47] 'Ilm-e-Akhlāq-e-Islamī, Volume 1, Page 435; Jāme' al-Sa'adāt, Volume 1, Page 357

Once, while wandering around, he came across a pious worshipper, above whose head flew a pigeon casting its shadow over him (thus protecting him from the sun). He said to himself: "I am a Banīshed person but this man is a pious individual; if I sit near him it is possible that due to his piety, Allāh may show mercy upon me too."

With this in mind, he approached the worshipper and sat down beside him. On seeing the exiled man sit next to him, the worshipper thought to himself: "I am the pious worshipper of this tribe whilst he is a disreputable, Banīshed and despised sinner; how can he sit down beside me?" Turning his head away from the man, the worshipper ordered him to go away from him.

Just as he had uttered these words, Allāh revealed to the prophet of the time: "Go to those two persons and ask them to start their deeds afresh, for I have forgiven all the sins of the immoral person and erased all the good deeds of the worshipper," (for exhibiting self-conceit and holding the other person in contempt).[48]

4 – The Short and Ugly Son

Ṣaʿdī narrates: "A king had several sons, one of them being short, thin and ugly, while the others were tall and good-looking.

The king would look at the short son with scorn and contempt, thereby causing him humiliation. The son, being intelligent, realized why his father looked down upon him and so said to him: "O' Father! A short but wise person is better than a tall but ignorant one. He who is taller is not necessarily better and superior; a sheep is clean but an elephant, like a carcass, always possess a foul smell."

The son's words made the king laugh and the elders of the court approved of what he said, but his brothers were upset.

[48] Shanīdani-hā-e-Tārīkh, Page 373; Maḥajjatul Baiḍā, Volume 6, Page 239

Coincidentally, during those days, it so happened that the enemy forces attacked the kingdom and the first person from the king's army to heroically attack the enemy was the king's short and ugly son. With a display of great courage, he felled a few of the enemy chiefs and then, returning to his father and paying his respects to him, said: "On the day of battle the lean horse comes of use."

Despite the fact that a group of his soldiers had taken flight, the son returned to the battlefield.

"O' Men! Endeavour hard or else put on the dress of womenfolk," he shouted with bitter sarcasm.

This sarcasm breathed fresh life into the cavalry who fought with renewed vigour till they eventually overcame the enemy forces and became victorious. The king kissed his son all over the face and named him his successor. From then on, he looked at this son with great respect and esteem. These events caused his brothers to become so envious of him that they put poison into his food in order to get rid of him. Fortunately, his sister watched what was happening through a small door and sent a warning signal to her brother by shutting the door loudly. The intelligent brother became suspicious and abstained from eating the food.

"It is impossible for skilled people to die while the unskilled ones continue to live on and take their place," he commented.

When the king was informed of the incident, he reprimanded the other brothers and sent each of them to the farthest part of his kingdom.[49]

[49] Hikāyat-hā-e-Gulistān, Page 43

5 - Bring forth One Worse than Yourself!

Allāh revealed to Prophet Mūsā عليه السلام: "The next time you come to converse with Me, bring along someone who is inferior to you."

Mūsā عليه السلام set out in quest of such a person but failed to find one, because every person that he encountered, he did not have the nerve to think that he was superior to that person.

Then, deciding to direct his search amongst the animals, his eyes fell upon a diseased dog. He decided to take it along with him. He tied a rope around the dog's neck and began pulling it but after a short distance, he regretted his action and set the dog free. He returned empty-handed to have his conversation with Allāh.

"Why did you not bring someone along with you, in accordance with My order?" came the voice from Allāh.

Mūsā عليه السلام beseeched, "O' Lord! I failed to find anyone who could be inferior to me."

The reply came from Allāh: "By My Might and Glory! Had you brought someone, regarding him to be inferior to yourself, I would have surely erased your name from the list of Prophets (and relieved you of the rank of Prophethood)!"[50]

---

[50] Namunah-e-Maʿarif, Volume 2, Page 676; Layālīul Akhbār, Page 197

26 – Pride

Allāh, the Wise, has said:

﴿ فَالَّذِينَ لاَ يُؤْمِنُوْنَ بِالآخِرَةِ قُلُوبُهُمْ مُّـــنْكِرَةٌ وَّ هُمْ مُسْــتَكْبِرُونَ ﴾

"As to those who believe not in the Hereafter, their hearts refuse to know, and they are arrogant." [51]

The Noble Prophet ﷺ said:

لاَ يَدْخُلُ الْجَنَّةَ مَنْ كَانَ فِي قَلْبِهِ مِثْقَالُ حَبَّةٍ مِنْ خَرْدَلٍ مِنْ كِبْرٍ.

"One, whose heart contains pride, (even if it is) in the measure of a mustard-seed, shall not enter Paradise." [52]

Short Explanation

A proud and arrogant person regards himself better and superior to others and by assuming vain and wishful thoughts in his mind, adopts the conduct of Shaitān (Satan) who said: "I have been created of fire while Adam has been created of earth, and fire possesses superiority over earth." The first sin to have been committed in the world of creation was arrogance on the part of Shaitān.

Thus, as for it being a vice, there can be no doubt or scepticism. Proud and arrogant individuals look down upon others and anticipate others to greet them and exhibit respect and deference towards them, always nurturing aspects of their superiority and greatness within their minds. The difference between ʿUjb and Takabbur is that someone who suffers from ʿUjb is egocentric, whereas one who suffers from takabbur possesses an air of self-superiority with respect to others and

---

[51] Noble Qur'an, Sūratul Naḥl (16) Verse 22

[52] Jāmeʿ al-Saʿadāt, Volume 1, Page 346

it is for this reason that his (spiritual) sickness is greater than one possessing ʿUjb.

1 – Abū Jahl

ʿAbdullāh Ibn Masʿūd, a companion of the Noble Prophet ﷺ, was the first person to openly recite the Qur'an in front of a gathering. He participated in all the battles of the Noble Prophet ﷺ but was so short that even when he stood up among people who were sitting, he would not rise above them! It was for this reason that in the battle of Badr, he requested the Noble Prophet ﷺ: "I do not possess the strength to fight in the battle; can you assign me some task by means of which I too can attain the same reward as those who fight?"

"Look amongst the dying infidels and if you happen to find anyone of them still alive, kill him," the Prophet ﷺ replied.

ʿAbdullāh narrates: "As I moved in the midst of people who seemed to be dead, I came to Abū Jahl, the most unyielding enemy of the Noble Prophet ﷺ. He still had some life left in him.

"I thank Allāh that He has humiliated you," I said as I sat on his chest.

Abū Jahl opened his eyes and grunted, "Woe unto you! Who has been victorious?"

"Victory is for Allāh and His Prophet, and it is for this reason that I shall kill you," I replied, placing my foot on his neck.

With great arrogance, he cried, "O' tiny shepherd! You have placed your foot on a very exalted place. Do know that nothing is more painful for me than to be killed by a dwarf like you. Oh! Why did not one of the sons of ʿAbdul Muṭṭalib kill me?"

I severed his head from his body and appeared before the Noble Prophet ﷺ.

"Glad tidings to you, O' Prophet of Allāh! This is the head of Abū Jahl."[53]

"Abū Jahl was more sinful and worse than Fir'awn of the time of Mūsā ﷺ. When Fir'awn was convinced that he would perish, he believed in Allāh, whereas when Abū Jahl became certain of his impending doom, he called upon Lāt and 'Uzza to save him," the Prophet remarked later.[54]

2 - Walīd Ibn Mughairah

Three years after having been appointed as a prophet and with only a handful of people having accepted Islam, it was revealed to the Noble Prophet ﷺ: "Openly proclaim your Prophethood and disregard the ridicule and troubles from the polytheists, for We shall protect you from their evils."

One of the opponents was Walīd Ibn Mughairah. Once, Jibra'īl the divine Archangel, was with the Noble Prophet ﷺ when Walīd happened to pass by. Seeing him, Jibra'īl asked the Noble Prophet ﷺ: "This Walīd Ibn Mughairah, is he of those who ridicule you?'

When the Noble Prophet replied in the affirmative, Jibra'īl pointed towards Walīd's foot.

Walīd continued walking until he reached the place where a person from the tribe of Khuza'ah was engaged in sharpening arrows. Walīd stepped on the sharp splinters and chippings lying on the ground, some of which penetrated into the heel of his foot. His heel was badly bruised as blood began to flow. Walīd's pride prevented him from bending down and plucking the splinters out of his heel. On reaching

[53] Paighambar Wa Yārān, Volume 4, Page 206; Tabaqāt Ibn Sa'd, Volume 3, Page 106

[54] Safīnatul Bihār, Volume 1, Page 200

his home, he heaved himself into a chair and dropped off to sleep while his daughter slept on the floor beside the chair.

Meanwhile, the blood gushed out so profusely from Walīd's wound that it reached the mattress of his daughter who woke up from her sleep. She asked her slave-girl why she had not shut the lid of the water-skin.

Walīd explained, "This is not the water from the water-skin. It is the blood of your father."

He then dictated his will and left this world - departing for Hell.[55]

3 – The Rich near the Poor

A rich person dressed in clean and elegant clothes arrived in the presence of the Noble Prophet ﷺ and sat down before him. A short while later, a poor person wearing old and tattered clothes, came and sat down near the rich person, who immediately gathered his neat garments from near the poor person and drew it towards himself.

Having observed this, the Noble Prophet ﷺ remarked to the rich man: "Did you fear that the poor person next to you might make your clothes dirty?"

"No," replied the man.

"Then why did you behave so?" asked the Noble Prophet ﷺ.

"I have a companion (soul) that makes good deeds appear evil to me and vice-versa. O' Prophet of Allāh! As a punishment for this reprehensible act of mine, I gift half of my wealth to the poor man".

Turning to the poor person, the Noble Prophet ﷺ inquired, "Do you accept the offer?"

"No, O' Prophet of Allāh," said the man.

---

[55] Muntahal Āʿmāl, Volume 1, Page 36

When the rich person wanted to know the reason, the poor man explained: "I fear I too might come to acquire the pride and self-conceit which has overwhelmed you."[56]

4 – Sulaīmān Ibn 'Abdul Mālik

One Friday, Sulaīmān Ibn 'Abdul Mālik, (one of the Caliphs of Banī Marwān) put on new clothes, applied perfume and ordered that the chest containing the royal turbans be brought before him.

With a mirror in one hand, he kept trying on one turban after another till he was eventually satisfied with one.

With pomp and glory, he set off for the mosque. As he entered the mosque, he ascended the pulpit, looking particularly pleased with his appearance, and kept adjusting his outfit. The sermon he delivered made him feel elated with himself and several times during the sermon, he appeared to be obsessed with his dress and thought to himself, "I am a Sultan, young, awe-inspiring and immensely generous."

At the end of his sermon, he descended from the pulpit and headed towards his palace. Once inside, he asked a female who seemed to be one of his slave-girls: "What is your opinion about me?"

"I find you to be honourable and joyous; alas! If only it were not for the poem of a poet!" replied the slave-girl.

Sulaīmān was taken aback by this comment. He insisted on hearing the poem, so she recited:

'You are a good commodity and investment, if only you remain forever,

But alas! For man, there is no eternity.'

---

[56] Rāhnama-e-Sa'ādat, Volume 1, Page 161; Al-Kāfī, Volume 2, Chapter The Excellence Of the Poor Muslims

As soon as Sulaīmān heard it, he burst into tears and continued to weep for the entire day. In the evening he summoned the slave-girl in order to find out what had prompted her to recite that poem, but she swore that till that day she had neither come before him nor had she recited any poem. All the other slave-girls vouched for her testimony. It then struck Sulaīmān that the incident had a supernatural dimension attached to it and the thought filled him with great fear and apprehension.

Not long afterwards, he departed from the world with the self-conceit that had come to seize him.[57]

5 – Khusrow Parvez

Of the kings to whom the Noble Prophet ﷺ had sent letters inviting them to Islam, one was Khusrow Parvez, the emperor of Iran. The letter was sent to him through ʿAbdullāh Ibn Hadhākah.

On receiving the letter, Khusrow ordered it to be translated. When it was translated, he noticed that the Noble Prophet ﷺ had written his own name before the emperor's and this proved too hard for him to digest. He tore the letter in fury, totally ignored ʿAbdullāh and refrained from responding to the letter.

When the Noble Prophet ﷺ was informed of this act, he prayed: "O' Lord! You too tear apart his kingdom."

Khusrow wrote to Bādhān, the king of Yemen: "It has reached my ears that a person has claimed Prophethood in Hijaz. Arrange to send two brave and courageous persons to him so that they may bring him to me as a captive."

Bādhān sent two persons, Bābwaih and KharkhʿAṣrah to Ḥijāz and they presented Bādhān's letter to the Noble Prophet ﷺ.

---

[57] Pand-e-Tārīkh, Volume 3, Page 37

He said to them: "You may rest now for I shall hand over my reply to you tomorrow."

The next morning when they arrived before him, the Noble Prophet ﷺ told them: "Inform Bādhān that last night (10th of Jumada al-Ulā, year 7 AH), when seven hours of the night had passed, my Lord killed Khusrow Parvez at the hands of his son Sheerwaih, and shortly we shall prevail over his empire. If you accept Islam, you can continue to rule over your region."[58]

[58] Dāstān-hā Wa Pand-hā, Volume 2, Page 126; Rauḍatul Safā

27 – Humbleness

Allāh, the Wise, has said:

﴿ وَ عِبَادُ الرَّحْمٰنِ الَّذِيْنَ يَمْشُوْنَ عَلَى الأَرْضِ هَوْناً ﴾

"And the servants of the Beneficent Allāh are they who walk on the earth in humbleness."[59]

The Noble Prophet ﷺ has said:

مَا تَوَاضَعَ أَحَدٌ لِلّٰهِ إِلاَّ رَفَعَهُ اللّٰهُ.

"There is none, who exhibits humility for (the sake of) Allāh, except that Allāh grants him greatness and eminence."[60]

Short Explanation

Humbleness is the root of all virtues. A humble person is always submissive before the majesty and greatness of Allāh, and lays the foundation of his acts of worship on the platform of this significant virtue.

None can comprehend the reality of humility except the Near Ones, from amongst the servants of Allāh who have comprehended the Unity of Allāh. Submissiveness and fear (with respect to Allāh) can only stem from humbleness and it is for this reason that the humble ones possess an appearance which causes them to be recognized by the angels and divine Gnostics.

Their appearance, demeanor, and social and domestic conduct clearly reveals that they are far away from every kind of pride and arrogance.[61]

---

[59] Noble Qur'an, Sūratul Furqān (25), Verse 63
[60] Jāmeʿ al-Saʿadāt, Volume 1, Page 359
[61] Tadhkeratul Ḥaqāiq, Page 55

1 – The Humbleness of Salmān Fārsī

Salmān had been the governor of one of the cities of Syria for some time. His conduct during the period of his rule remained unchanged from that before his governorship; he would always wear ordinary clothing, travel on foot and even place his household things as security and surety (for borrowing money).

Once, while moving through the bazār, he saw a man who had purchased some alfalfa and was looking for someone to carry it to his house for him. Salmān approached the person, who failed to recognize him, and agreed to carry his load free of charge. The man placed the load of alfalfa on Salmān's back. As they were walking, they came across a person who immediately recognized Salmān.

"O' Leader! Where are you carrying this burden?" he exclaimed.

Hearing these words, the owner of the load realized that the person carrying his load was Salmān. He fell down on his knees and implored: "Forgive me, for I had failed to recognise you."

"Nevertheless, I must carry this load to your house," said Salmān.

When he had done so, he said to the man, "I have fulfilled my promise; now it is for you to promise that henceforth you will never seek the services of anyone for anything. (And know!) By you carrying things which you are able to, it will not reflect negatively upon your manliness."[62]

2 – Bilāl the Abyssinian

Bilāl was one of those Muslims who had made great progress spiritually to the extent that he became the muezzin of the Noble Prophet ﷺ. The Noble Prophet ﷺ would say to him: "O' Bilāl! Invigorate my soul (by means of your Adhān)."

[62] Jawāme' al-Hikāyāt, Page 178

The Noble Prophet ﷺ not only placed him in charge of the public treasury, but also treated him as if he were his blood brother.

"When I enter Paradise, I shall hear your footsteps ahead of me, as you walk on its lush-green ground," he had told Bilāl.

Consequently, the other Muslims would approach Bilāl and congratulate him for the lofty rank that he had come to acquire for himself, but he never allowed their compliments to make him arrogant, nor did he permit the people's praises to change him. With great humbleness, he would respond to their praises by saying, "I am an Abyssinian and (till yesterday) I had been a slave."[63]

3 - The Humbleness of the Noble Prophet

Abū Dharr narrates: "Once, I observed Salmān and Bilāl arriving in the presence of the Noble Prophet ﷺ. Salmān, out of respect, fell down at the Prophet's feet and kissed them. The Noble Prophet ﷺ endeavoured to prevent him from performing this act.

"Do not perform acts that the non-Arabs perform for their emperors," advised the Noble Prophet ﷺ. "I am (just) a servant from amongst the servants of Allāh - I eat what they eat and sit where they sit."[64]

4 - Muḥammad Ibn Muslim

Muḥammad Ibn Muslim was a wealthy individual from the nobles of Kufah and a companion of Imām Bāqir عليه السلام and Imām Ṣādiq عليه السلام. Once, Imām Bāqir عليه السلام advised him: "O' Muḥammad! You must be humble and modest."

[63] Hikāyat-hā-e-Shanīdani, Volume 4, Page 173; Tabaqāt Ibn Sa'd, Volume 3, Page 238

[64] Dars-hai Az Zindagi-e-Payāmbar, Page 162; Biḥārul Anwār, Volume 76, Page 63

On his return to Kufah from Madinah, Muḥammad Ibn Muslim picked up a pair of scales and a container of dates. He then sat down at the door of Kufah's main mosque and began calling out: "Whoever needs dates, should purchase them from me." (He acted thus so that not the slightest pride should remain within him).

His relatives objected to him by saying that he had disgraced them through this act of his.

"My Imām has instructed me to perform a task and I shall not disobey him; I shall not move from this place till I have sold all the dates that are in this container," said Muḥammad.

"If it is as you say, then you might as well take up the work of a miller," his relatives said to him sarcastically.

To their surprise, Muḥammad agreed. He purchased a hand-mill and busied himself with grinding wheat into flour, the intention being to emancipate himself from vanity and self-importance.[65]

5 – ʿIsā and the Washing of his Disciples' Feet

ʿIsā Ibn Maryam ﷺ once told his disciples that he sought a favour from them.

"What do you want us to do?" they asked.

ʿIsā ﷺ moved from his place and washed the feet of all the disciples!

"O' Spirit of Allāh! It is more befitting that we should wash your feet!" they exclaimed.

"The person who is the most deserving to serve is one who is a scholar. I have acted thus in order that I may have demonstrated humbleness. You too should develop the quality of humbleness and

[65] Riwāyat-hā Wa Hikāyat-hā, Page 103; Dāstān-hā-e-Parākandeh, Volume 3, Page 18

after I have gone you should behave with the people with humility and modesty just as I have behaved with you,"

ʿIsā ﷺ said. "It is by means of humbleness and not arrogance that wisdom flourishes, just as it is on soft ground that plants grow, not on hard mountainous terrain."[66]

[66] Namunah-e-Maʿarif, Volume 3, Page 223; Al-Wāfī, Volume 1, Page 4

28 – Repentance

Allāh, the Wise, has said:

﴿ وَ أَنِ اسْتَغْفِرُوا رَبَّكُمْ ثُمَّ تُوبُوا إِلَيْهِ ﴾

"And that you ask forgiveness of your Lord, then turn to Him."[67]

Imām Ṣādiq ﷺ said:

إِذَا تَابَ الْعَبْدُ تَوْبَةً نَصُوحاً أَحَبَّهُ اللّٰهُ فَسَتَرَ عَلَيْهِ.

"If a servant repents sincerely, Allāh loves him (and) so conceals his sins."[68]

Short Explanation

Repentance is the cord of Allāh which those repenting must necessarily grasp; they need to clean their interior of their sins and testify against themselves before their Lord.

They should be repentant from the depths of their hearts with regards to their past misdeeds, and fearful with regards to the remaining period of their lives. The auliya (friends) of Allāh repent for the (inappropriate) thoughts that may have passed through their minds, while the special ones repent for engaging themselves in anything other than Allāh, even as the general masses repent for the sins committed by them.

It is vital that, in order to make amends for past (mis)deeds and refrain from committing sins in the future, the person repenting should not look upon any sin as being trivial and insignificant, but should always

---

[67] Noble Qur'an, Sūrat Hūd (11), Verse 3
[68] Jāmeʿ al-Saʿadāt, Volume 3, Page 65

experience regret over his past lapses, keep his soul away from various kinds of lust and guide it towards struggle (against lust) and worship.[69]

1 – The Inventor of A Religion and Repentance

Imām Ṣādiq ﷺ related: "In ancient times there lived a man who sought to earn his livelihood and procure great wealth by lawful means but was unsuccessful. He then strived to achieve his objectives by unlawful means but once again failed.

Satan appeared before him and said to him: "You tried to acquire great wealth by lawful as well as unlawful means but were unsuccessful. Do you want me to show you a way by which you would not only become wealthy but you would also attract numerous followers?"

The man expressed his willingness to know how he could get rich.

"Concoct a religion and invite people to follow it," suggested Satan.

The man fabricated a religion and soon, he had a lot of followers through whom he became rich.

One day he realized that he had made a mistake by leading numerous people astray so he resolved to inform the people of the falsity of his religion and the error of his ways. But however hard he stressed and emphasized, the people simply refused to accept his word.

"Your previous views were correct; have you become sceptical of your own religion now?" they asked. When he heard these words, he got some shackles and chained himself. He pledged that he would not unchain himself until Allāh accepted his repentance.

Allāh revealed to the Prophet of the time to convey the following message to the person: "By My Honour! Even if you weep and supplicate to the extent that every ligament of your body falls apart, I shall never accept your prayers, till you inform those people who have

[69] Tadhkeratul Ḥaqāiq, Page 75

died after having been led astray by you of the reality and they turn back from your religion."[70]

2 – The Employee of Banī Umayyah

ʿAlī Ibn Hamzah relates: "I had a young friend who worked as a scribe within the Banī Umayyah administration. Once, he asked me to arrange an appointment for him to meet Imām Ṣādiq ﷺ. I sought permission from the Imām ﷺ and he agreed to meet the man. At the appointed time, my friend and I arrived in the Imām's ﷺ presence.

My friend greeted the Imām ﷺ, sat down and said: "May I be made your ransom! I had occupied a position in the Ministry of Treasury of the Banī Umayyah and have managed to acquire great wealth, although I have committed some crimes too!"

"If the Banī Umayyah did not have people like you to collect taxes for them and accompany them in their battles, they could not have usurped our rights," said Imām Ṣādiq ﷺ.

"Does there exist a way for my salvation?" pleaded the youth.

The Imām ﷺ asked: "If I tell you, would you act upon it?"

The youth replied in the affirmative.

"From the possessions that remain with you, return those whose owners are known to you, and as for those things for which the owners are unknown to you, give them off in charity on behalf of their owners. In exchange for this act, I shall guarantee you Paradise!" said Imām ﷺ.

Lowering his head, the youth responded after a long deliberation: "May I be made your ransom! I shall do as instructed by you."

ʿAlī Ibn Hamzah says: We got up and proceeded towards Kufah. There, my friend divested himself of all his possessions - even his clothes -

[70] Pand-e-Tārīkh, Volume 4, Page 251; Biḥārul Anwār, Volume 2, Page 277

either returning them to their owners or giving them to charity. I collected some money from my friends to purchase some clothes for him and I used to send him money for his expenses.

A few months after this incident, he fell ill and we used to visit him regularly during his sickness. One day, when I paid him a visit, I found him on the verge of dying. Opening his eyes he said to me: "O' ʿAlī! The Imām ﷺ has fulfilled his promise." Then he departed from the world. We performed the ablutions, shrouded his body and finally buried him.

Some time later, I visited the Imām ﷺ. As soon as his eyes fell upon me, he said: "O' ʿAlī! I have fulfilled my promise to your friend."

"May I be made your ransom! It is as you say. He too mentioned it (the guarantee of Paradise) to me before his death," I said."[71]

3 – Return before Death

Muāʿwiyah Ibn Wahab narrates: "When we set out for Makkah, there was an old man with us who used to engage himself in acts of worship, but did not profess the Shiʿite faith. This old man was accompanied by his nephew, who was of the Shiʿites.

During the journey, the old man fell sick. I said to his nephew: "Why don't you inform him of the true faith; it is possible that Allāh may take him away from the world in the state of true faith and Wilāyah."

However, the other people advised him to leave the man alone and to let him die upon his own faith. However his nephew did not heed their advice. He went to his uncle and said: "O' Uncle! After the death of the Noble Prophet ﷺ, the people, with the exception of a handful who had adhered to Amīrul Mo'minīn ﷺ, became apostates despite

[71] Shanīdani-hā-e-Tārīkh, Page 55; Maḥajjatul Baiḍā, Volume 3, Page 254

the fact that the Caliphate (of Amīrul Mo'minīn ﷺ) had already been stipulated by the Noble Prophet ﷺ."

Hearing these words, the old man heaved a sigh and said, "I accept this faith," and then breathed his last."

Muāʿwiyah Ibn Wahab relates: "We entered Madinah and arrived before Imām Ṣādiq ﷺ. ʿAlī Ibn Sarī, one of our companions, related the incident of the old man's repentance and his acceptance of Imāmate just before his death, to the Imām ﷺ who said: "He is of the inmates of Paradise."

ʿAlī Ibn Sarī remarked in astonishment: "The old man did not know anything about our faith and was totally ignorant of its laws and rulings; it was only when his soul was about to separate from his body that he accepted this faith!"

The Imām ﷺ explained: "What (more) do you want of him? By Allāh! He has (already) entered Paradise."[72]

4 – Abū Lubābah

Abū Lubābah was one of the distinguished companions of the Noble Prophet ﷺ and had participated in the battle of Uhud and the conquest of Makkah. One of the sensitive aspects of his life was the incident of his repentance.

When the tribe of Banī Quraidhah violated their covenant with the Noble Prophet ﷺ, the Noble Prophet ﷺ initiated a military expedition against them and besieged their fort. Some persons from the tribe of Aus approached him and requested: "Just as you had handed over the fate of the tribe of Banī Qainaqaʿa to be decided by the tribe of Khazraj, leave it upon us to decide the fate of the tribe of Banī Quraidhah."

[72] Khazīnatul Jawāhir, Page 312; Rauḍatul Anwār of Sabzwārī

"Will you be satisfied if I were to appoint one person from your tribe to rule in the matter?" the Noble Prophet ﷺ asked.

They agreed. The Noble Prophet ﷺ suggested Sa'd Ibn Mu'ādh, but the Banī Quraidhah refused to accept him. They told him to send Abū Lubābah to them so that they could confer with him. The Noble Prophet ﷺ assigned Abū Lubābah, who had his house, property and family in the fort of Banī Quraidhah, the task of conducting consultations with them.

As soon as Abū Lubābah entered the fort, men and women, old and young, surrounded him and began lamenting and complaining to him (over the state of affairs) with the intention of attracting his pity and compassion. Then they asked: "Should we submit before the rule of the Noble Prophet ﷺ?"

"You could do that," he replied, making a gesture (by pointing to his neck) to indicate that submission was equivalent to death.

He quickly realized that by performing this act, he had been unfaithful and disloyal to the Noble Prophet ﷺ. It was on this occasion that the following verse was revealed: "O you who believe! Be not unfaithful to Allāh and the Messenger, nor be unfaithful to your trusts while you know. Know that your property and your children are a temptation, and that Allāh is He with Whom there is a mighty reward."[73]

Overcome with shame, he came out of the fort and proceeded straight towards the mosque of Madinah and, tying himself to one of its pillars in the mosque, called out: "None should untie me till Allāh accepts my repentance."

[73] Noble Qur'an, Sūratul Anfāl (8), Verse 27-28

يا أَيُّهَا الَّذِينَ آمَنُوا لا تَخُونُوا اللَّهَ وَ الرَّسُولَ وَ تَخُونُوا أَماناتِكُمْ وَ أَنْتُمْ تَعْلَمُونَ وَ اعْلَمُوا أَنَّما أَموالُكُم وَ أَولادُكُم فِتنَةٌ وَ أَنَّ اللهَ عِندَهُ أَجر عَظِيم

He remained in that state for ten to fifteen days, allowing himself to be untied only for prayers or to go to the washroom.

"If Abū Lubābah had come to me, I would have sought forgiveness for him but since he himself awaits Allāh's forgiveness, leave him alone till Allāh forgives him," the Noble Prophet ﷺ commented when he came to know what Abū Labābah had done.

Umme Salamah states: "One day, at dawn, I saw the Noble Prophet ﷺ happy and smiling. May Allāh always keep you smiling! What is the reason for it?" I asked him.

"Jibra'īl has informed me that Abū Lubābah's repentance has been accepted," he said.

"Do I have your permission to inform him of the good news?" I asked.

"You may if you wish," he answered. From inside the room I called out: "Glad tidings, O' Abū Lubābah! Allāh has accepted your repentance."

The people rushed forward to untie him but he ordered: "I place you under the oath of Allāh that none, except the Noble Prophet ﷺ, should untie me."

When the Noble Prophet ﷺ arrived in the mosque for the morning prayers, he untied Abū Lubābah from the pillar which stands even today, in the Mosque of the Noble Prophet ﷺ and is popularly known as the 'Pillar of Repentance' or the 'Pillar of Abū Lubābah'.[74]

---

[74] Paighambar Wa Yārān, Volume 1, Page 129; Majma' al-Bayān, under the discussion regarding verse 102 of the chapter al-Taubah:

وَ آخَرُونَ اعْتَرَفُوا بِذُنُوبِهِمْ خَلَطُوا عَمَلاً صالِحاً وَ آخَرَ سَيِّئاً عَسَى اللّهُ أَنْ يَتُوبَ عَلَيْهِمْ إِنَّ اللّهَ غَفُورٌ رَحِيمٌ

5 – Buhlūl[75], the Gravedigger

Muʿādh Ibn Jabal was in tears when he arrived in the presence of the Noble Prophet ﷺ and greeted him. The Noble Prophet ﷺ replied to his greeting and asked: "What makes you cry?"

"At the door of the mosque, there is a good-looking youth who weeps as intensely as a mother whose young son has died, and he wishes to meet you," replied Muʿādh.

The Noble Prophet ﷺ agreed to meet him.

The youth entered and greeted the Noble Prophet ﷺ who returned his greeting and enquired: "Why do you weep?"

"Why should I not weep? I have committed sins which Allāh will never forgive and He is bound to hurl me into Hell," said the youth.

"Have you associated someone with Allāh?"

"No."

"Have you killed anybody?"

"No."

"Even if your sins are of the magnitude of mountains, Allāh shall forgive them," said the Noble Prophet ﷺ.

"My sins are greater than the mountains," the youth explained.

"Are your sins in the magnitude of the seven earths, the seas, the sands, the trees, all that lies on the earth, in the skies, the stars, the Throne and the Chair?" asked the Noble Prophet ﷺ).

"My sins are greater than all of these things."

"Woe unto you! Are your sins greater than your Lord?"

---

[75] Editor's note: Not to be confused with Buhlūl who lived during the time of Imām Riḍā عليه السلام.

The youth lowered his head and replied, “Allāh is devoid of all blemishes; it is my Lord, who is greater.”

“Would you not relate one of your sins to me?” enquired the Noble Prophet ﷺ.

“Why not?” responded the youth, whose name was Buhūl. “For seven years I used to dig up the graves of the dead, take out their shrouds and sell them. One night, a maiden from amongst the Anṣār (The Helpers) died and was buried in the cemetery. When I dug open her grave to remove the shroud from her body, the Satan tempted me and I committed a grave sin. As I was turning back, the body called out to me: “O’ Youth! Don’t you fear the Ruler of the Day of Judgment? Woe unto you of the fire of the Day of Judgment!”

Having narrated this, the youth wanted to know what he should do.

“O’ Sinner! Stay away from me for I fear that I might burn in your fire too!” cried out the Noble Prophet ﷺ.

The youth left, heading straight towards the mountains. He tied his hands to his neck and became engrossed in worship, supplications and seeking forgiveness.

For forty days, he wept day and night to the extent that even the wild beasts were affected by his weeping. After forty days he asked Allāh to either punish him by means of fire or forgive him, so that he might not have to face humiliation on the Day of Judgment.

Allāh revealed the following verse, which refers to the forgiveness of Buhūl: “And those who, when they commit an indecency or do injustices to their souls, remember Allāh and ask forgiveness for their faults... and who forgives the faults but Allāh.”[76]

[76] Holy Qur’an, Surah Āle ‘Imrān (3), Verse 135:

وَ الَّذينَ إِذا فَعَلُوا فاحِشَةً أَوْ ظَلَمُوا أَنْفُسَهُمْ ذَكَرُوا اللَّهَ فَاسْتَغْفَرُوا لِذُنُوبِهِمْ وَ مَنْ يَغْفِرُ الذُّنُوبَ إِلاَّ اللَّهُ

The Noble Prophet ﷺ recited this verse with a smiling face and then asked: "Who can take me to that youth?"

Muʿādh agreed to take him. Accompanied by Muʿādh, the Noble Prophet ﷺ went to the place where the youth was. He saw him standing between two boulders, hands tied to his neck and engaged in supplication. His face had become dark due to the scorching sun and all his eyelashes had fallen off due to the intense weeping. Wild beasts had gathered around him while the birds circled over his head, all of them weeping over his distressed and pitiable state.

The Noble Prophet ﷺ advanced towards him, untied his hands and cleared the soil from the top of his head.

"O' Buhūl! Glad tidings for you; you have been liberated by Allāh from the fire (of Hell)," he said.

Then, turning to his companions, he said, "This is how you should make amends for your sins."[77]

[77] Risālah Liqāullāh, Page 62; Majālis as-Ṣadūq

29 – Ignorance

Allāh, the Wise, has said:

﴿ خُذِ الْعَفْوَ وَ امُرْ بِالْعُرْفِ وَ أَعْرِضْ عَنِ الْجَاهِلِينَ ﴾

"Take to forgiveness and enjoin good and turn aside from the ignorant."[78]

Imām ʿAlī عليه السلام has said:

أَلْجَهْلُ أَصْلُ كُلِّ شَرٍّ.

"Ignorance is the root of all evils."[79]

Short Explanation

Ignorance is a state that exists within humans and one who possesses it advances towards darkness, whereas one who keeps it away from himself reaches luminosity and acquires discernment and insight.

If a person chooses an incorrect path for himself and permits ignorance to guide him in his actions, he would be looked upon as a sinner and of the inmates of Hell. However, if he sets about on the correct path, and acts on the basis of knowledge and cognizance, he shall be of the delivered ones.

Being pleased and satisfied over one's actions is the key that opens the door of ignorance and the worst trait of an ignorant person is to claim to possess knowledge despite being ignorant.

An ignorant person, upon noticing his own faults, does not experience uneasiness and discomfort, and upon being advised, does not pay heed to it. Despite having knowledge of his ignorance (called simple ignorance) he still commits blunders.

---

[78] Noble Qur'an, Sūratul Ā'rāf (7), Verse 199

[79] Ghurar al-Ḥikam, Tradition 819

1 – The Ignorant Commander

Yaʿqūb Laith Saffār (d. 265 AH) had a commander by the name of Ibrāhīm who despite being brave and courageous, was extremely ignorant.

Once during winter, Yaʿqūb ordered that his personal winter clothes be given to Ibrāhīm. Ibrāhīm had a servant by the name of Aḥmad Ibn ʿAbdullāh, who had hatred towards him. When Ibrāhīm returned home, Aḥmad asked him: "Don't you know that whomsoever Yaʿqūb Laith gives his personal clothes, he puts that person to death within that week?"

"Oh no! I was not aware of this. What is the way out?" asked Ibrāhīm.

Aḥmad suggested to him that he should flee from there. He even agreed to accompany Ibrāhīm and arranged to meet him the following day. Later, Aḥmad secretly went to Yaʿqūb Laith and informed him that Ibrāhīm was intending to flee to Sīstān from where he would initiate a rebellion against Yaʿqūb Laith. Yaʿqūb pondered for a while and was on the verge of ordering his army to prepare for battle with Ibrāhīm when Aḥmad made a request.

"Allow me to single-handedly bring Ibrāhīm's severed head before you," he said to Yaʿqūb.

Yaʿqūb Laith agreed. As Ibrāhīm was about to leave the city with his soldiers, Aḥmad attacked him from behind, severed his head with his sword and brought it before Yaʿqūb Laith. Yaʿqūb handed the position of Ibrāhīm, his ignorant commander, to Aḥmad who thus came to enjoy great esteem in his eyes.[80]

[80] Namunah-e-Maʿārif, Volume 4, Page 93

2 – The Caliph's Ignorant Son

Mahdī ʿAbbāsi, the third ʿAbbāsid Caliph, had a son by the name of Ibrāhīm, who was a misguided individual. He showed intense enmity and malice towards Amīrul Mo'minīn عليه السلام in particular.

Once he approached Maʿmun, the seventh ʿAbbāsid Caliph, and said to him:

"I saw ʿAlī عليه السلام in my dream. We were travelling together till we reached a bridge whereupon he granted me precedence in crossing it. I said to him: 'You claim to be the Commander of the Faithful, but we are more deserving of this status'. ʿAlī عليه السلام did not give me a proper answer."

"How did he answer you?" Mamun questioned.

"He simply greeted me several times by saying 'Peace, Peace'," replied Ibrāhīm.

"By Allāh! He has answered you loud and clear," explained Maʿmun. Ibrāhīm was puzzled. Maʿmun went on, "He viewed you as an ignorant person, unworthy of responding to. This is because Allāh, describing His special servants in the Qur'an, says: "And the servants of the Beneficent Allāh are they who walk on the earth in humbleness, and when the ignorant address them, they say: Peace,"[81] which is (an expression) indicative of their lack of regard (with respect to the ignorant ones) and their (personal) greatness.

"ʿAlī عليه السلام looked upon you as an ignorant person and behaved with you as the Qur'an has recommended when dealing with ignorant persons."[82]

---

[81] Noble Qur'an, Sūratul Furqān (25), Verse 63: وَ إذا خاطَبَهُمُ الْجاهِلُونَ قالُوا سَلاماً

[82] Hikāyat-hā-e-Shanīdani, Volume 2, Page 20; Safīnatul Bihār, Volume 1, Page 79

3 – The Handsome but Ignorant Person

A pleasant, dignified looking person entered the court of Abū Yūsuf Kufi (d. 182 AH), the judge of Hārūn Rashīd who regarded him with great respect. The person sat in the gathering with such silence and dignity, that it prompted the judge to regard him as a person of great virtue. He asked the man if he wanted to say something.

"I seek an answer to a question," said the person.

"Whatever I know, I shall answer you," responded the judge humbly.

The person enquired, "When can a person break his fast?"

"When the sun sets," replied the judge.

"What if the sun does not set till midnight?"

Hearing this, the judge laughed out and said, "How appropriately has the poet Jarīr Ibn ʿAtiyyah (a poet of the Umayyad period, who had died in the year 110 AH) said:

Silence is a beauty for a person who is weak and ignorant[83]; surely, the intelligence of a person is known by his speech, just as his lack of intelligence also becomes manifest as a result of his speech."

Thus, the judge came to know of the ignorance of the good-looking person.[84]

4 – Qais Ibn ʿĀṣim

Qais Ibn ʿĀṣim was a tribal leader during the Age of Ignorance but he later accepted Islam.

Once, during his old age, in order to seek ways to make amends for his past misdeeds, he arrived in the presence of the Noble Prophet ﷺ and said: "In the past, ignorance had instigated numerous fathers to bury

[83] وَ فِي الصَّمتِ زينٌ لِلْغَبِي

[84] Latāif al-Tawāf, Page 412

their innocent daughters alive. I too, had buried twelve of my daughters alive at short intervals. My wife gave birth to my thirteenth daughter in secret and, making it appear to me as if it had been a stillborn child, she secretly sent the infant to her own relatives (for upbringing).

Years passed till one day I returned home suddenly and unexpectedly from one of my trips, only to find a small girl in my house. Since she resembled my children, I found myself perplexed till eventually I came to know that she was my daughter.

I immediately took hold of the girl, who was weeping profusely, and took her to a remote location, refusing to permit myself to be affected by her wailing. She kept pleading, 'I shall return to my maternal uncles and shall never come to your house again', but I paid no heed to her request and buried her alive."

When he had narrated this, Qais noticed that tears flowed down the Noble Prophet's ﷺ eyes and heard him murmuring: "One who does not look upon others with mercy shall not be looked upon with mercy."[85]

Then turning to Qais, he said, "You have difficult days ahead of you!"

"What should I do to lessen the burden of my misdeeds?" inquired Qais.

"For every daughter killed, set free a slave-girl," replied the Noble Prophet ﷺ.[86]

---

[85] مَن لاَ يَرْحَم لاَ يُرْحَم

[86] Dāstān-hā Wa Pand-hā, Volume 1, Page 15; Jāhiliyyat Wa Islam, Page 632

5 – A Long Beard

Jāhidh Baṣrī, (d. 249 AH) who has a book to his name in every branch of science, states: "Ma'mun 'Abbāsi and a few other individuals had gathered together and were engaged in conversation.

"A person who sports a long beard is stupid and foolish," one of them remarked.

Some others objected by saying, "On the contrary, we have seen individuals growing long beards but who were clever and intelligent."

"Impossible!" exclaimed Ma'mun.

At that moment, a man with a long beard and riding a camel came towards them. Ma'mun, in order to prove his point, summoned the person and asked him what his name was.

"Abū Hamdwaih", replied the man.

"What is your agnomen?" asked Ma'mun.

"'Alawiyyah."

Ma'mun said to those around him, "A person who is so ignorant so as to be unable to differentiate between a name and an agnomen, all his other acts would also be characterized with the same ignorance."

Turning to the man once again, he asked, "What work do you do?"

"I am a jurisprudent and an expert in various sciences. If the king desires, he can question me."

"A person sold a sheep to another person, who took the animal in his possession. But he had not yet paid the price of the animal when it released its dung, which fell into the eyes of another person, blinding him. Under the circumstances, whose obligation is it to pay the compensation for the injury caused?" asked Ma'mun.

The person with the long beard reflected for a while and then said: "The compensation should be paid by the seller and not the purchaser." Those around wanted to know why.

"It is because the seller did not inform the purchaser that he had placed a catapult inside the rear of the sheep, which it used for hurling stones in order to protect itself," explained the person.

Hearing this, Ma'mun and those around him burst out in laughter. The man was given some money and he left.

"The truth of my statement has become manifest before you that the elders have stated[87]: A long-bearded person is a dimwit," said Ma'mun.[88]

[87] There are traditions that censure the keeping of a long beard. One of the things, which Imām 'Alī ﷺ mentioned in his criticism of the people of Baṣrah, was their long beards. The Noble Prophet ﷺ regarded not sporting a long beard as being one of the felicities of man. (Safīnatul Bihār, Volume2, Page 509)

[88] Jawāme' al-Ḥikāyāt, Page 300

30 – Greed

Allāh, the Wise, has said:

﴿ إِنَّ الإِنْسَانَ خُلِقَ هَلُوْعاً ﴾

"Surely man is created of a hasty temperament."[89]

The Noble Prophet ﷺ said:

يَشِيْبُ ابْنُ آدَمَ وَ تَشُبُّ فِيهِ خَصْلَتَانِ: أَلْحَرْصُ وَ طُوْلُ الأَمَلِ.

"(As) man becomes old, two attributes in him turn young - greed and lofty aspirations."[90]

Short Explanation

If man is greedy in acquiring things, he shall not possess the proximity of Allāh, since he has abandoned the attribute of tawakkul (trust in Allāh), is not content with what Allāh has appointed for him and has adopted hastiness, which is an attribute of Satan.

Allāh has created the world similar to a shadow; following the shadow yields nothing except for exhaustion and fatigue. If one seeks the world in excess of what is necessary, not only does he not acquire it but also suffers troubles and hardships.

The Noble Prophet ﷺ has said: "A greedy person (always) remains excluded." And an excluded person is hated and reproached.

A greedy person's thoughts are disturbed and his troubles numerous - constantly involved in seeking and computing riches, neither at peace in this world nor inclined towards the Hereafter.[91]

---

[89] Noble Qur'an, Sūratul Maʿārij (70), Verse 19
[90] Jāmeʿ al-Saʿadāt, Volume 2, Page 100
[91] Tadhkeratul Ḥaqāiq, Page 33

1 – The Mud from a Grave is a Greedy Person's Medicine

Ṣaʿdī relates: "I had heard that a trader who owned forty slaves and one hundred and fifty camel-loads of goods used to travel from city to city for the purpose of trade. One night, on the island of Kish, he invited me into his room.

I went to his room but throughout that night, he was restless. He kept rambling on ceaselessly and would say: "Such and such storeroom of mine is in Turkistan, a certain cargo of mine is in India, this is the deed of sale of a particular land, another cargo is held up due to some merchandise, such and such person is the guarantor for a loan... I am contemplating travelling to Alexandria, but the Mediterranean Sea is stormy at the moment...

O' Ṣaʿdī! I have another journey before me, which if I were to accomplish, I would spend the rest of my life in solitude and never embark upon any more journeys, ever."

"Which is that journey after which you will never undertake any other journey?" I asked him.

He replied, " I wish to take Iranian sulphur to China, for I have heard that it sells at a very high price there; from China, I shall take porcelain bowls to Rome; in Rome I shall purchase the exquisite Roman silk for selling it in India; in India, I shall take Indian iron to Halab (Syria) from where I shall purchase the Halabi mirror and glass, and proceed towards Yemen; there, I shall purchase Yemeni clothes and bring them to Iran after which I shall quit travelling and settle down to manage a shop."

He continued on to such an extent that he was eventually overcome with exhaustion and, unable to speak any more, he said to me: "O' Ṣaʿdī! Tell me what you think of what you have just heard."

I said, "You surely know that at a very far place from the land of Ghour (between Hirāt and Ghaznah) when a trader fell off his mount and died, a person commented: "Only two things can satiate a greedy world-loving person - contentment or the earth of a grave."[92]

2 – Greedy for Pleasure

Yazīd Ibn 'Abdul Malik (the tenth Umayyad caliph) became caliph after 'Umar Ibn 'Abdul 'Azīz. Contrary to his predecessor, he used to engage himself, day and night, in feasting, festive gatherings, drinking and merry-making in the company of two of his slave-girls, Salāmah and Habābah, who were beautiful singers.

Habābah eventually brushed aside her rival Salāmah and took the reins of the caliph in her hands.

Maslamah Ibn 'Abdul Mālik, approached his brother Yazīd and said: "'Umar Ibn 'Abdul 'Azīz was extremely just whereas you, in contrast, drink and engage yourself in various pleasures and have handed over the kingdom to a singer, Ḥabābah. Moreover, while the people are keen to catch a glimpse of you, you have dropped yourself into her arms. Leave her aside and pay attention to the affairs of the caliphate."

Yazīd resolved to heed his brother's counselling and decided to lead the Friday prayers. Meanwhile, Ḥabābah had instructed her slave-girls to inform her the moment the caliph stepped out. As soon as the slave-girls informed her that the caliph had come out, she appeared before him and, with a lute in hand and in a melodious and enchanting voice, recited the following poem: "If an enamoured one has lost his intelligence, do not censure him; the poor thing is exhibiting patience due to the intensity of his anguish."

[92] Hikāyat-hā-e-Gulistān, Page 166

The caliph, seeing his beloved one in that engaging state and hearing her captivating voice, covered his face with his hands.

"Ḥabābah! Enough! Stop it!" he cried and then recited the following poem: "Life is nothing except living luxuriously and gratifying oneself; even if the people censure you."

And then he shrieked: "O' the beloved of the beloved ones! You have spoken the truth. May Allāh destroy anyone who criticizes me for being in love with you! O' Slave! Go and ask my brother Maslamah to go to the mosque and lead the prayers in my place."

He then headed towards his pleasure-hall first, and later, for greater fun and enjoyment, proceeded towards Bait al-Rass, which is situated near Damascus. Once there, he said to his slaves: "People think that there is no pleasure without any bitterness and I wish to prove the falsity of this notion of theirs."

He remained there in order that no news or letters ever reached him. He remained completely engrossed in merry-making without the slightest of troubles.

However, as fate would have it, one day a seed of pomegranate got stuck in Ḥabābah's throat and, following a bout of severe coughing, she passed away. Day and night, the caliph held the lifeless body of Habābah in his arms and shed tears over it, and it was only on the insistence of her relatives that her stinking body was eventually buried. The caliph too, after this incident, did not live for more than fifteen days and was laid to rest near the grave of Habābah.[93]

3 – ʿIsā and the Greedy Person

Prophet ʿIsā ﷺ had been travelling in the company of another person when, after having journeyed for a period, they were overcome by

[93] Rahnamā-e-Saʿādat, Volume 3, Page 657; Tārīkh-e-Tamaddun-e-Islam, Volume 1, Page 86

hunger. They reached a village where ʿIsā ﷺ requested his companion to go and bring some bread, while he engaged himself in prayers.

The man returned with three loaves of bread and waited for ʿIsā ﷺ to join him, but since his prayers continued for a long time, the person quietly consumed one loaf of bread.

"Were there three loaves of bread?" ʿIsā ﷺ asked after completing his prayers.

"No, there were only two," replied the man.

A short while after they had eaten their food, they set off again and on the way encountered a herd of deer. ʿIsā ﷺ summoned one of the deer towards him, sacrificed it, and both the men sat down to eat it. When they had finished eating, ʿIsā ﷺ commanded: "O' deer! Move by the permission of Allāh!" The deer immediately came to life and sprinted away.

Witnessing this, the man stood dumbfounded and uttered, "Subhānallāh (Glory be to Allāh)."

"I put you under the oath of He, Who has manifested this sign of His power before you! Tell me what happened to the third loaf of bread?" ʿIsā ﷺ asked him.

"There were only two loaves of bread!" the man insisted.

They continued on their journey and soon reached the outskirts of a large village where they happened to see three gold bricks lying before them.

"There appears to be great wealth here!" the man remarked.

"Yes. One brick is for you, the second for me and I shall hand over the third to the person who ate the third loaf of bread," said ʿIsā ﷺ.

The greedy man blurted out, "I ate the third loaf of bread."

'Isā عليه السلام parted company with him and handing him the bricks, said: "All three bricks are your property now."

The man sat down beside the gold bricks and was lost in thought as to how he would carry them and put them to good use, when three persons passed by. When their eyes fell upon the gold bricks, they killed the man and took possession of the bricks. As they were hungry, they decided that one of them would go to the nearby village and arrange to get some bread. The person who had gone to get the bread, thought to himself: "I shall poison the bread so that the other two are killed and then I shall have all the three bricks for myself."

In the meantime, his other two friends had also conspired to kill him upon his return so that they could divide his share of the bricks between themselves. When he returned, they killed him as planned and with great satisfaction in their actions, began eating the bread. Before long they too died as a result of the poison contained in the bread.

On his return, 'Isā عليه السلام, observing four dead persons lying near the three gold bricks remarked[94]: This is how the world conducts itself with those who covet it.[95]

4 – Dhul Qarnain[96]

[94] هَكَذَا تَفعَلُ الدُّنْيَا بِأهلِهَا

[95] Pand-e-Tārīkh, Volume 2, Page 124; Anwārul Nu'māniyah, Page 353

[96] His name has been mentioned in Sūratul Kahf of the Noble Qur'an; he is the same Alexander, of the progeny of Prophet Nūḥ عليه السلام who had traveled to the east and the west of the world and constructed the city of Alexandria. Since he used to gather his hair in the form of two horns near his forehead, he came to be popularly known as Dhul Qarnain, - 'The possessor of two horns'. He lived for nearly two centuries and had conquered around 36 countries all over the world.

Dhul Qarnain, during the course of his journey, reached Dhulumāt, where he came across a palace in which he noticed a youth standing there dressed in white, face raised towards the skies and his hands placed upon his lips.

The youth, upon seeing him, asked him who he was.

"Dhul Qarnain," came the reply.

The youth (who was the angel Israfeel) said to him, "When the Day of Judgment arrives, I shall blow the Trumpet." Then, picking up a stone and handing it to Dhul Qarnain, he said, "If this stone becomes satiated, you too shall become satiated and if this stone happens to be hungry, you too shall be hungry!"

Dhul Qarnain carried the stone to his friends and placed it on a scale in order to weigh it, but despite weighing against a thousand similar stones, it still weighed more than all of them taken together.[97]

At that moment, Prophet Khidhr ﷺ came to them; placing a stone on the opposite scale, he put some earth over the stone when suddenly, all of them observed that the scales had balanced perfectly. Dhul Qarnain wanted to know the reason for this from Prophet Khidhr ﷺ, who explained: "Allāh wished to admonish you that in spite of conquering so many nations, you are still not satisfied; man can never become satiated except when a handful of earth is dropped over his face, and nothing can fill his stomach except earth."

Dhul Qarnain began to weep and turned back.

On another occasion, he came across a man sitting near a grave and fiddling with some decayed bones and decomposed skulls that lay before him. He asked the man what he was doing.

---

[97] It had been a supernatural act, performed to jolt Dhul Qarnain into awareness and lead him towards subservience and obedience of Allāh.

The man replied, "I want to separate the bones of the kings from those of the poor ones but find myself unable to do so."

Dhul Qarnain passed by and thought to himself, "That act of his was intended for me."

He then settled down in Daumah al-Jandal[98], abandoned his quest for global conquest and engaged himself in Allāh's worship.[99]

5 – Ash'ab Ibn Jubaīr Madanī (d. 154 AH)

He was a person who was squint-eyed, bald on two sides of his head and unable to pronounce the letters ر (rā) and ل (lām). He possessed such intense greed for material wealth and food that he never seemed to be fully satisfied in this regard. When questioned about this attribute of his, he replied: "Each time I see smoke bellowing out of someone's house, I feel as if they are preparing the food for me and I sit waiting for the food. But when, despite waiting for a very long time, there is no sign of any food, I dip dry bread in water and eat it!

And whenever I hear the adhān being recited over a deceased, I feel that the deceased has set aside one third of his wealth for me and with this thought in mind, I go to his house and assist in giving him the ablutions, covering him in his shroud and, finally participating in his burial. But when after his burial there is no sign of the wealth, I return home disappointed and dejected.

And when I walk through the streets, I spread my cloak apart in the hope that perhaps a person, while throwing a thing from his roof or window to his neighbour, may slip-up and that thing may land in my cloak."

[98] Fakhr Rāzī states: Dhul Qarnain returned to Iraq and fell sick in the city of Zur, where he eventually passed away. (Safīnatul Bihār, Volume 2, 426)

[99] Namunah-e-Ma'ārif, Volume 4, Page 234; Layaliul Akhbār, Page 46

It is said that once while passing through a street, he came across some children engaged in playing games. He decided to tell them a lie.

"O' Children! Why do you stand here when at a crossroad further down there is a person distributing his load of red and white apples amongst the people for free?" he told them.

Hearing this, the children immediately rushed towards the crossroad. As they ran, Ashʿab was himself overcome with greed and he too started to run towards the crossroad.

"You have fabricated the story yourself, so why do you run?" the people asked him.

He replied, "The children ran out of seriousness whereas I run out of greed. Maybe there is really someone out there distributing the apples and I do not wish to remain deprived of them."[100]

[100] Latāif al-Tawāif, Page 361

31 - Envy

Allāh, the Wise, has said:

﴿ أَمْ يَحْسُدُونَ النَّاسَ عَلىٰ ماَ آتَاهُمُ اللّٰهُ مِنْ فَضْلِه ﴾

"Or do they envy the people for what Allāh has given them of His grace?"[101]

Imām Ṣādiq ﷺ has said:

إِنَّ الْمُؤْمِنَ يَغْبِطُ وَ لاَ يَحْسِدُ.

"A true believer exults, but never envies."[102]

Short Explanation

Envy stems from blindness of the heart and rejection of Allāh's grace – the two wings of kufr and disbelief. An envious person's evil afflicts him before it can afflict the envied; just like Iblees, whose evil overtook his own self and made him the eternally accursed one, whereas Adam went on to attain the rank of Prophethood.

The balance (of deeds) of a jealous person is light, thereby making Hell his abode, whereas the balance (of deeds) of the envied person is heavy, thereby leading him to Paradise. In view of this, Qābeel, who had murdered his brother Hābeel because of this vice, hurled himself in Hell while sending his brother to Paradise.

If this vice penetrates into the soul of a person, he would never be able to repent (for his misdeeds) but instead, would always be on the lookout to cause harm and injury to those, who are either superior to him or possess more than him.[103]

---

[101] Noble Qur'an, Sūratul Nisā (4), Verse 54

[102] Jāme' al-Sa'adāt, Volume 2, Page 195

[103] Tadhkeratul Ḥaqāiq, Page 49

1 – The Friend of ʿIsā

Imām Ṣādiq عليه السلام said: "Stay away from jealousy and do not harbour envy with respect to one another." Having said this, the Imām عليه السلام continued: "One of the practices which Prophet ʿIsā عليه السلام adopted for himself, was to travel from city to city. During one of these journeys, he took along with him a companion who was of short build and who also happened to be one of his attendants.

After a while, they reached the sea. ʿIsā عليه السلام recited the name of Allāh, stepped onto the water and began walking over it effortlessly. Repeating what ʿIsā عليه السلام has performed, the companion recited what the prophet had and began to follow him over the water. In the middle of the sea he thought to himself, "ʿIsā is a prophet and walks over water and I am walking over water too, so what superiority does he possess over me?"

These thoughts hardly crossed his mind when he suddenly fell into the water and began to plead to ʿIsā عليه السلام for help.

ʿIsā عليه السلام took hold of his hand and pulled him out of the water.

"What did you say that caused you to fall into the water?" he asked. The companion confessed to the thoughts that had passed through his mind.

"You placed yourself in a position other than what Allāh had ordained for you, thus becoming the object of His wrath," remarked ʿIsā عليه السلام. "Seek forgiveness so that you regain your previous rank once again."

As soon as the companion sought forgiveness, he began to follow ʿIsā عليه السلام over the water once again."

After narrating this incident, Imām Ṣādiq عليه السلام advised: "Fear Allāh and avoid jealousy."[104]

---

104 Shanīdani-hā-e-Tārīkh, Page 316; Maḥajjatul Baiḍā, Volume 5, Page 328

2 – 'Abdullāh Ibn Ubayy

As the people of Madinah were accepting the Noble Prophet ﷺ in increasing numbers, 'Abdullāh Ibn Ubayy, one of the Jewish elders, became even more envious towards the Noble Prophet ﷺ, and thus planned to kill him.

He invited the Noble Prophet ﷺ, 'Alī عليه السلام and the other companions for his daughter's wedding-feast. Meanwhile, he had a huge pit dug up in the courtyard of his house, filled its base with swords, arrows and lances, and had it covered up with a carpet. In addition to this, he poisoned the food and also concealed some Jews, armed with poisoned swords, in the house. His idea was that when the Noble Prophet ﷺ and his companions walked towards the pit, they would fall into it whereupon the armed Jews would rush out and put them to death. He had poisoned the food so that should this plan fail, they would be killed by means of the poison.

Jibra'īl, through the orders of Allāh, revealed these two plans which stemmed from jealousy and envy to the Noble Prophet ﷺ and said to him: "Your Lord says: Go to 'Abdullāh Ibn Ubayy's house and sit wherever he requests you to sit and eat whatever he presents before you, for I shall suffice you and protect you from his evil designs."

The Noble Prophet ﷺ, Amīrul Mo'minīn عليه السلام and the other companions entered 'Abdullah's house. 'Abdullāh ushered them to the courtyard of his house. As per his request, all of them sat over the pit but nothing happened, much to 'Abdullāh's astonishment.

He then ordered the poisoned food to be brought. When it was placed before them, the Noble Prophet ﷺ told 'Alī عليه السلام to recite the following over the food: "In the name of Allāh, The Healer; in the name of Allāh, The Sufficient; in the name of Allāh, The Acquitter; in the name of Allāh, with Whose name no thing or sickness, in the earth or in the heaven, can cause harm, and He is the All-Hearing, the All-Knowing."

Then, all of them ate the food and came out of the gathering without being harmed in the slightest. ʿAbdullāh's bewilderment knew no bounds; he assumed that the food had not been poisoned and so ordered the armed Jews to eat it, as a result of which, all of them died.

Meanwhile, his daughter who was the bride, decided to sit down on the carpet covering the pit. As soon as she did so, she plummeted into the pit. Her shrieks filled the air, only to subside with her death.

ʿAbdullāh ordered his servants not to reveal the cause of all the deaths in the house. When the news of these incidents reached the Noble Prophet ﷺ, he asked the jealous ʿAbdullāh what had happened.

"My daughter fell off the roof of the house; as for the others, they died due to diarrhoea," he replied.[105]

3 – The Strange Act of the Envious Person

During the caliphate of Hādī ʿAbbāsi[106], there lived in Baghdad a wealthy person who was righteous and beneficent. In his vicinity, there resided a person, who was envious of his wealth, and no matter how much he tried to taint the wealthy person's prestige and bring him into disrepute, he could not succeed. Finally, he decided to purchase a slave, train him and then use him to implement his evil intention.

One day, after a year had passed, he asked his slave: "How obedient are you to your master?"

The slave replied, "If you ask me to hurl myself into the fire, I shall do so." The man was overjoyed to hear this.

"My neighbour is rich and wealthy and I bear animosity towards him. I want you to carry out my instructions. Tonight, both of us shall

---

[105] Khazinah al-Jawāhir, Page 344; Biḥārul Anwār, Volume 6

[106] He was the brother of Hārūn al-Rashīd and was the caliph for almost a year after which, the caliphate reached Harūn.

climb onto the roof of his house where you will kill me so that he is accused of my murder and is put to death by the government as a punishment for killing me," he said to the slave.

However much the slave insisted on not carrying out these instructions, it was to no avail and the man remained unyielding. At midnight, as per the orders of his envious master, the slave severed his master's head on top the roof of the rich neighbour and hurried back to his bed.

The next day, the death of the jealous person came to light and Hādī ʿAbbāsi had the rich person arrested, and subjected him to interrogation. He then summoned the slave and interrogated him too.

The slave, observing that the rich person was totally innocent, divulged the incident of jealousy and the subsequent killing. Hearing the incident, the Caliph lowered his head, reflected for a while and then raised it again.

"Although you have killed a person, you exhibited courage and saved an innocent person from accusation, therefore, I shall set you free," the Caliph said to the slave.

In this manner, the harm of envy and jealousy rebounded upon the envious person himself.[107]

4 - The Envy of the Womenfolk

Ibn Abī Laila was the judge during the caliphate of Manṣūr Dawāniqī.

"Many strange and interesting cases are brought before the judges and it is my desire that you relate one of them to me," Manṣūr said to him.

[107] Dāstān-hā-e-Mā, Volume 2, Page 138; Mustadrakul Wasāʾil, Volume 3 (In the biography of Faḍlullāh Rāwandī)

Ibn Abī Laila related: "One day an old and humble lady approached me and implored me to defend her right and punish her oppressor. I asked her who she wanted to complain about.

She replied, "My niece."

I ordered the niece to be brought before me. When she arrived, I observed that she possessed charming looks and an appealing physique. I asked her the reason for her aunt's complaint whereupon she related the entire case as follows: "I am the daughter of this old woman's brother and she is my aunt. My father died while I was still a child and this aunt of mine took care of me and was never negligent with respect to my upbringing. When I grew up, with my consent, she married me to a goldsmith.

My comfortable life made my aunt envious of me. She ornamented her daughter and brought her before my husband, who became captivated by her and sought her hand in marriage.

This aunt of mine stipulated that she would marry her daughter to him only if the authority to retain or divorce me was placed in her hands. My husband agreed to this condition.

"After a period, my aunt had me divorced and I separated from my husband. Meanwhile, my aunt's husband, who had been away on a journey, returned home. After realising what had happened, he used to console me. I presented myself to him in such a manner that he found me attractive. Eventually, he fell for me and expressed his desire to marry me.

I said to him, "I shall only agree upon the condition that the authority of divorcing my aunt be placed in my hands."

"He agreed and after the marriage, I had my aunt divorced and I continued to live with this husband, who died after a period of time.

One day, my first husband approached me and expressed his inclination to marry me again.

"I am willing to marry you again but upon the condition that you should grant me the authority to either retain or divorce my aunt's daughter," I told him.

He accepted and once again I got married to my first husband and, with the authority vested in me, I also had my aunt's daughter divorced.

Now you can judge that I have committed no offense; all that I have done is to recompense the baseless envy of this aunt of mine." [108]

5 – The Consequence of Jealousy

Once, during the Caliphate of Muʿtasim ʿAbbāsī, a learned person arrived in his court.

Muʿtasim was so impressed with his talks and speeches that he ordered him to come to the court every few days. The man used to come regularly and before long became one of the confidants of the Caliph. Another of the Caliph's confidants became jealous of this person and fearing that he would take over his ministry, considered ways of getting rid of him.

One day, at the time of Dhuhr, as he was leaving the Caliph's gathering together with the learned person, he requested him to accompany him to his house so that they could talk and have lunch together. The learned man accepted his request.

When they sat for lunch, garlic was also served with the food and the man consumed a lot of it. At the time of ʿAṣr, the jealous person proceeded towards the Caliph and said: "As I am burdened by your favours and bounties, I cannot conceal this secret from you. This

[108] Pand-e-Tārīkh, Volume 2, Page 156; Iʿlām al-Nās (of Atlidī), Page 44

learned man who is your confidant, has been secretly complaining to the people that the foul odour from the Caliph's mouth is killing him but the Caliph repeatedly summons him to go to him."

The Caliph was horrified to hear this and ordered the learned man to be brought before him. Since he had consumed a lot of garlic, he covered his mouth with a handkerchief and sat at a distance from the Caliph. Observing this, the Caliph became certain of the truthfulness of the minister's words. He wrote a letter to one of his assistants instructing him to kill the bearer of that letter and he asked the learned man to take it to the assistant.

The jealous confidant was waiting outside the room. As soon as the man came out of the Caliph's court with the letter in his hand, the confidant thought that the letter contained the Caliph's orders for a large sum of money to be given to him, and this added fuel to his already flaming envy. He offered two thousand dirhams to the man in return for the letter. The learned man accepted the money and also accepted the confidant's request not to go to the Caliph for a few days.

The jealous confidant took the letter to the Caliph's assistant who immediately beheaded him. Some days later, the Caliph enquired, "Where is the learned man? Has he gone on a journey?"

Those around him said, "No, we have seen him just recently." The Caliph ordered that he be brought before him. When he had arrived, the Caliph, with great astonishment, inquired: "I had given you a letter to hand over to my assistant, did you not do as instructed?"

The man recounted the incident of the letter and the jealous minister.

The Caliph said, "I shall ask you a question; do not lie. Did you tell my confidant that the foul odour from the Caliph's mouth troubled you?" The learned man replied in the negative.

"Why then did you sit away from me when you last came to see me and covered your mouth with a handkerchief?" asked the astounded Caliph.

"Your confidant had taken me to his house and fed me garlic and so when I arrived in your presence, I feared lest the odour should inconvenience you," replied the man.

Hearing this, the Caliph uttered, "Allāhu Akbar!" and then related the whole incident to those present around him. All of them were left astonished and amazed.[109]

[109] Rangārang, Volume 1, Page 358

32 - Truth and Falsehood

Allāh, the Wise, has said:

﴿ قُلْ جَآءَ الْحَقُّ وَ زَهَقَ الْبَاطِلُ اِنَّ الْبَاطِلَ كَانَ زَهُوْقاً ﴾

"And say: The truth has come and the falsehood has vanished; surely falsehood is a vanishing (thing)."[110]

Imām ʿAlī عليه السلام said:

ظَلَمَ الْحَقَّ مَنْ نَصَرَ الْبَاطِلَ.

"One, who helps falsehood, has oppressed (and done injustice to) the truth."[111]

Short Explanation

There are several levels to comprehending truth and falsehood, and individuals differ vastly with respect to acceptance and rejection of them. The general rule, with regards to the truth, is that the heart should be inclined towards Allāh, His commandments and the realities, while the rule with regards to falsehood, is that the heart should be averse to things that are prohibited and related to other than Allāh, and the interior should be kept away from dirty and impure carnal attachments.

A pious person comprehends that falsehood weans a person away from realities and it shall cease to exist, and it is only truth, which is deep-rooted and continues to exist. Thus, one must adhere to the people of truth and stay away from the people of falsehood.

---

110 Noble Qur'an, Sūratul Isrā (17), Verse 81
111 Ghurar al-Ḥikam, Tradition 6041

1 – The Right of a Deceased Muslim

Zurārah relates: I was in the company of Imām Bāqir عليه السلام in the funeral procession of a person from Quraish. ʿAtā, the jurist of Makkah, was amongst those present in the funeral procession. Suddenly, the air was filled with the wailing of a lady. ʿAtā instructed her to remain quiet as otherwise he would have to turn back. But the lady continued to wail and so ʿAtā left the procession.

I informed the Imām عليه السلام about ʿAtā's turning back.

"Why?" inquired the Imām عليه السلام.

I replied, "Due to the lamentation of a lady. He asked her to keep quiet and when she did not, he left."

Imām Bāqir عليه السلام said, "Stay with me and we shall accompany the deceased. If we notice falsehood together with the truth and forsake the truth due to that falsehood, we would not have fulfilled the right of the Muslim." i.e. escorting the funeral of the Muslim, which is his right, should not be forsaken for the sake of the wailing of that lady (which, according to the non-Shi'ite sects, is forbidden and prohibited).

When the prayers were offered for the dead person, his relative said to the Imām عليه السلام: "May Allāh have mercy upon you! You can turn back for you do not possess the strength to walk." Imām عليه السلام continued to accompany the funeral procession.

Zurārah continues: I said to Imām Bāqir عليه السلام, "The relative of the deceased has permitted you to turn back."

"If you have some work, you may go," said the Imām عليه السلام. "I have neither come here with his permission nor do I need his permission to return. I have come here to seek the rewards, since man shall be rewarded in the measure in which he accompanies a funeral procession." [112]

2 – Muā'wiyah Ibn Yazīd

After the three-year Caliphate of Yazīd (who brought about the murder of Imām Ḥusain ﷺ), the lootings and crimes in Madinah and sacrilege with respect to the Ka'bah, the Caliphate reached his son Muā'wiyah. Whenever Muā'wiyah slept at night, two slave-girls would remain awake, one near his head while the other near his feet, in order to protect him from inconveniences.

One night, thinking that the Caliph was asleep, the slave-girls began conversing with each other.

"The Caliph likes me more than you and if he does not set his eyes upon me three times a day, he gets restless and disturbed," the one that sat near the Caliph's head said.

"Hell is the abode for both of you," commented the other slave-girl.

Not being able to sleep, Muā'wiyah heard the conversation. Predictably, he felt the urge to get up and put the slave-girl to death, but he controlled himself and waited to hear more of their dialogue.

The first slave-girl wanted to know why the second one had made that remark. She got the following reply: "Muā'wiyah and Yazīd, the grandfather and father of this Muā'wiyah, were the usurpers of the Caliphate, since the rank was the right and privilege of the household of the Noble Prophet ﷺ."

When Muā'wiyah heard this, he drifted into deep reflection and finally made up his mind to step down from the false Caliphate and inform the people of the true leader.

---

112 Bā Mardum In Guneh Barkhord Konīm, Page 55; Al-Kāfī, Volume 3, Page 171

The next morning he ordered all the people to be present in the mosque. When the mosque was full, he ascended the pulpit and after praising Allāh, said: "O' People! The Caliphate is the right of Imām Sajjād ﷺ whereas my grandfather, my father and I were its usurpers."

He descended from the pulpit, returned to his house, locked himself in and refused to allow anyone to enter it. When his mother was informed of the incident, she approached him, beating her head with her hands.

"Oh! How I wish that you had been the blood of my monthly cycle so that I might not have had to witness such an act from you!" she shouted.

Muā'wiyah remarked, "By Allāh! I wish I had been just what you desired so that you had never given birth to me!"

For forty days he did not emerge from his house. In the meantime, Marwan Ibn Hakam took over the reins of the Caliphate. Marwan then married Muā'wiyah's mother (Yazīd's wife) and a few days later he had Muā'wiyah poisoned.[113]

3 – Accepting the Truth

One night, Sa'īd Ibn Mūsāyyab entered the mosque of the Noble Prophet ﷺ wherein he observed a person offering prayers. He was reciting them in a loud and beautiful voice. Sa'īd instructed his slave to go to the person and request him to recite his prayers softly.

"The mosque is not our property; this person has a right over it too," the slave said.

Sa'īd decided to do it himself. He called out in a loud voice: "O' Worshipper! If you are offering your prayers for Allāh, then lower

[113] Dāstān-hā Wa Pand-hā, Volume 9, Page 154; Jāme' al-Nuraīn, Page 316

your voice, but if you are offering it for the people, (then do realize) they shall not benefit you in the least."

The person, appreciating the truth in this advice, lowered his voice and recited the remainder of the prayers in a low voice. As soon as he had completed his prayers, he picked up his shoes and left the mosque. After he had left, it transpired that the person was 'Umar Ibn 'Abdūl 'Aziz, the ruler of Madinah.[114]

4 - The Intoxicated turns Grateful

Dhunnūn Miṣrī relates: "I had come out of Egypt for a walk and was strolling along the banks of the river Nile gazing at its water, when I suddenly caught glimpse of a scorpion moving forward hastily. I wondered where it was heading. As it reached the riverbank, a frog surfaced from within the water; the scorpion climbed onto its back and the frog began to swim through the water. "There is something mysterious about this event," I thought to myself. I jumped into the water and began to swim after them.

I observed that when the frog had reached land, the scorpion got down from his back. I continued to follow the scorpion till I reached a tree. There, I found a youth lying in its shade. Beside him was a black snake that was about to bite him. Suddenly, the scorpion rushed forward and stung the snake in the back. The snake died instantly.

After this, the scorpion proceeded towards the water, climbed onto the frog's back and was ferried to the other side. I stood absolutely amazed.

"This person is surely one of the auliya (close friends) of Allāh!" I whispered. I was about to kiss his feet when I realized that the man was intoxicated, and this only served to add to my amazement. I

[114] Shanīdani-hā-e-Tārīkh, Page 18; Maḥajjatul Baiḍā, Volume 2, Page 230

waited patiently for the youth to recover from his drunken state and when he regained consciousness, he saw me standing near him.

"O' one, who is the leader of his time! You have come near this sinner and honoured him," he exclaimed in astonishment.

I told him to leave aside the rhetoric but to look at the snake beside him. Seeing the snake near him, he slapped his forehead and inquired what had happened. I related to him the entire incident of the scorpion, frog and the snake. On hearing about this and observing the grace of Allāh upon him, he raised his head towards the heaven and cried: "O' You! If Your grace upon the intoxicated ones is in such measure, how much would it be upon (Your) friends?"

Then, after performing ablution in the Nile, he turned towards his house. From then on, he engaged himself in self-rectification, till he reached such a stage and rank that every sick person for whom he prayed would become cured."[115]

5 – The Gratitude of Abū Dharr

When Abū Dharr received the news that a Prophet had manifested himself in Makkah, he instructed his brother Anīs to go and acquire some information about him.

His brother went to Makkah, came back and described the Noble Prophet ﷺ to him.

"You have not been able to smother the flames that smolder within my heart," Abū Dharr complained.

He therefore made arrangements to undertake a journey to Makkah. On his arrival there, he took shelter in one corner of a mosque till on the third day, under the guidance of ʿAlī ؑ, he covertly approached the Noble Prophet ﷺ and greeted him.

[115] Jawāmeʿ al-Hikāyāt, Page 46; Siyar as-Ṣāliḥīn

When the Noble Prophet ﷺ asked him his name and inquired about him, Abū Dharr gave him the answers, following which he accepted Islam.

The Noble Prophet ﷺ advised him: "Return to your city and do not stay in Makkah for I fear that you might be subjected to persecution (here)."

"By He, in Whose Hand lies my soul! I shall shout out in front of the people and loudly proclaim my acceptance of Islam," responded Abū Dharr.

He headed straight towards Masjidul Ḥarām where in a loud voice, he testified to the Unity of Allāh and the Prophethood of the Noble Prophet ﷺ. Hearing this, the people of Makkah rushed towards him to beat him up till he dropped down, unconscious. As ʿAbbās, the paternal uncle of the Noble Prophet ﷺ witnessed the scene, he threw himself upon Abū Dharr and shouted out to the people: "O' People! Woe unto you! Do you not see that this person is from the tribe of Ghaffar and was amidst you while on a journey towards Syria?" With these words, he managed to save Abū Dharr's life.

The next day, his condition improved but Abū Dharr again proclaimed his new faith and was badly beaten up once more. For the second time in as many days, ʿAbbās intervened and saved him from their beatings. After this, Abū Dharr left Makkah and returned to his city.[116]

[116] Paighambar Wa Yārān, Volume 1, Page 45; Āʿyān al-Shīʿa, Page 316

33 – Lawful and Unlawful

Allāh, the Wise, has said:

﴿ يَا أَيُّهَا النَّاسُ كُلُوا مِمَّا فِي الأَرْضِ حَلاَلاً طَيِّباً ﴾

"O mankind! eat the lawful and good things out of what is in the earth."[117]

Imām Kaẓim عليه السلام said:

إِنَّ الْحَرَامَ لاَ يُنْمِي وَ إِنْ نُمِيَ لَمْ يُبارَكْ فيه.

"Surely, the unlawful things do not grow (and multiply) and if they ever do, they are never blessed."[118]

Short Explanation

Consumption of lawful things results in soundness of health and a good Hereafter, whereas consumption of unlawful things causes hardening of the heart - the gravest of diseases for the heart. Its ill effects are also seen to manifest in one's progeny and even becomes cause for a person to stand up in opposition to Allāh! The Prophets and the auliya never ate unlawful things and always counseled their ummah to earn a lawful income and desist from unlawful things.

Why should one who shall eventually be in need of only a grave and a few meters of shroud strive to collect wealth by unlawful means only to leave it for the others, not to mention its burden and responsibility?

In regards to earning a lawful income, it has been reported from the Noble Prophet ﷺ that worship consists of seventy parts, the most excellent of them being the earning of a lawful income. The act of

---

[117] Noble Qur'an, Sūratul Baqarah (2), Verse 168

[118] Jāmeʿ al-Saʿadāt, Volume 2, Page 167

earning a lawful income causes a person's heart to become illuminated, his acts of worship to be accepted, and the person finds himself in the continuous protection of Allāh.[3]

1 – The Jews and the Unlawful Food

When the Noble Prophet ﷺ was seven years of age, the Jews (having perceived signs of Prophethood in him and therefore deciding to test him) discussed amongst themselves: "We have read in our Scriptures that the Prophet will distance himself from unlawful and dubious food, so let us test him."

Thus, they stole a fowl and gifted it to Abū Ṭālib so that the members of his family could eat it. All of them ate, except for the Noble Prophet ﷺ who did not touch the food. When questioned, he replied: "This fowl is unlawful and Allāh has protected me from unlawful things."

After this incident, the Jews got hold of a neighbour's fowl with the intention of paying him later and sent it to Abū Ṭālib, but once again the Noble Prophet ﷺ refused to eat the food, saying: "This food is dubious (with respect to its lawfulness)."

When the Jews came to know of these incidents, they commented, "This child shall come to possess a lofty rank and status."[119]

2 – By Unlawful Means

During the period when Imām Bāqir عليه السلام was in the captivity of Manṣūr Dawāniqi (the second ʿAbbāsid Caliph), he used to eat very little food. Once, a righteous lady who was the follower of the Ahlul Bayt prepared two loaves of bread by lawful means and sent it to the Imām عليه السلام so that he could eat them. The jail warden said to Imām عليه السلام:

---

[3] Safīnatul Bihār, Volume 1, Page 297

[119] Dars-hāi Az Zindagi-e-Payāmbar, Page 31; Bihārul Anwār, Volume 15, Page 336

"A certain pious lady, who happens to be your follower has sent these loaves as a present for you and has sworn that it has been made out of lawful means and has requested you to eat them."

The Imām ﷺ refused to accept the loaves and asked for them to be returned to the lady.

"Tell her: We know that your food is lawful; however, since you have made it reach us by unlawful means, it does not befit us to eat it," he said.[120]

3 - The Satan's Snare

One of the students of Āyatullāh Sheikh Murtaḍā Anṣāri recounts: "One night, while we were in Najaf engaged in studies under the tutelage of the Sheikh, I saw Shaitān in my dreams. He was armed with numerous ropes and cords in his hands.

"What are these ropes for?" I asked him.

He replied, "I put them around people's necks, draw them towards myself and ensnare them. Just last night, I had put one of these strong cords around the Sheikh's neck and had managed to drag him from his room to the middle of the street in which his house is situated, but unfortunately he escaped from my clutches and returned home."

The next morning when I went to the Sheikh, I related the previous night's dream to him.

"Shaitān has spoken the truth," the Sheikh explained. "That accursed had desired to beguile me but by the grace of Allāh, I escaped from his grasp. Yesterday, I did not have any money to purchase something for the house. I said to myself: 'I have one riyal from the money of Imām al-Zamān ﷺ and there is still some time before I can put it to use. I shall borrow it for now and repay it later.'

[120] Latāif al-Tawāif, Page 44

"I left the house with that money, but as I was about to purchase the item which I needed, I said to myself: "How do I know I shall be able to repay this debt later?" I wavered and then all of a sudden decided against going ahead with the purchase. As soon as I returned home, I put the money back in its place."[121]

4 – The Caliph's Food

Once, in a gathering of Hārūn Rashīd (the fifth ʿAbbāsid Caliph), which included a number of aristocrats, the conversation drifted towards Buhūl and his insanity.

When it was time for lunch, a king's luncheon was spread out, and a delicacy especially prepared for Hārūn was placed before him. Hārūn handed this food to one of his slaves and ordered him to take the food to Buhūl, in the hope of drawing him towards himself with this benevolent act.

When the slave brought the food before Buhūl, who was seated in the ruins of a broken down house, he noticed that some dogs nearby were tearing apart and eating the carcass of a dead donkey. Buhūl refused to accept the food.

"Place the food before the dogs," he said to the slave.

"This is the Caliph's special food and he has sent it to you out of his respect for you. Do not insult the Caliph!" ordered the slave.

Buhūl responded, "Lower your voice for if the dogs come to know of this, even they would refuse to eat this food." (Since, with regards to the riches at the Caliph's disposal, it is not known which part of it is lawful and which part is not.)[122]

---

[121] Sīmā-e-Farzānegān, Page 430; Zindagānī Wa Shakhsiyyat-e-Sheikh Anṣārī, Page 88

[122] Ḥikāyat-hā-e-Shanīdani, Volume 1, Page 120

5 – 'Aqīl

Once, ʿAqīl, the brother of Imām ʿAlī عليه السلام, seeking some monetary help, asked the Imām عليه السلام to give him something because he was poor.

The Imām عليه السلام said, "Be patient till I distribute the money amongst the other Muslims for then, I shall give you your share too."

But when ʿAqīl persisted with his request, the Imām عليه السلام said to a person: "Take ʿAqīl by the hand towards the market and ask him to force open the lock of one of the shops and take away everything from it!"

ʿAqīl immediately asked, "You want me to be arrested as a thief?"

"And by giving you money from the public treasury of the Muslims you want me to be looked upon as a thief?" the Imām عليه السلام retorted.

"I shall go to Muāʿwiyah," replied ʿAqīl.

Imām ʿAlī عليه السلام suggested to him to do as he pleased. ʿAqīl went to Muāʿwiyah to seek help from him whereupon Muāʿwiyah gave him a hundred thousand dirhams and said: "Ascend the pulpit and inform the people as to how ʿAlī عليه السلام behaved with you and how I cooperated with you."

ʿAqīl climbed up the pulpit and, after thanking and praising Allāh, said: "O' People! When I sought from ʿAlī عليه السلام his religion, he abandoned me - his brother, and adhered to his religion. However, when I approached Muāʿwiyah, he gave me preference over his religion."[123]

[123] Pand-e-Tārīkh, Volume 1, Page 180; Al-Sawāiqul Muhriqah

34 – Forbearance

Allāh, the Wise, has said:

﴿ إِنَّ إِبْرَاهِيْمَ لَحَلِيْمٌ أَوَّاهٌ مُّنِيبٌ ﴾

"Most surely Ibrāhīm was forbearing, tender-hearted, oft-returning (to Allāh)."[124]

Imām Ṣādiq عليه السلام had said:

إِذَا لَـــمْ تَكُنْ حَلِيماً فَتَحَلَّمْ

"If you are not forbearing then portray yourself as one possessing forbearance."[125]

Short Explanation

Forbearance is Allāh's lantern from the illumination of which a person achieves the proximity of Allāh. A forbearing person, in the face of ill treatment by his family, friends and other people, exhibits patience for the sake of divine pleasure. The reality of forbearance is when a person, despite having the power and ability to extract revenge, pardons the person who has caused him harm and injury; we read in the supplications: "O' Lord! Your grace is (too) expansive and Your forbearance is (too) immense that You should punish me for my deeds and disgrace me for my sins."

Since the significance of a true believer more than anyone else, thus, it is imperative for him to exhibit forbearance in the face of troubles and inconveniences of the foolish ones, for if he were to stand up in

---

124 Noble Qur'an, Sūrat Hūd (11), Verse 75

125 Jāmeʿ al-Saʿadāt, Volume 1, Page 297

confrontation with them, it would be tantamount to adding fuel to the fire and only serve to aggravate the issue.[126]

1 – The Nuisances of the Pigeon-Fancier

Sheikh Abū ʿAlī Thaqafī had a neighbour who loved pigeons. His pigeons would perch on the roof of the Sheikh's house and in order to make them fly away, he would fling stones at them, an act that caused disturbance and inconvenience to the Sheikh.

One day, the Sheikh was sitting in his house reciting the Noble Qur'an, when the neighbour hurled a stone at the pigeons. The stone struck the Sheikh on his forehead, injuring him and causing blood to flow down his forehead.

The Sheikh's companions were overjoyed and spoke amongst themselves: "Tomorrow, the Sheikh is bound to complain to the governor of the city and we shall soon be relieved of the pigeon-fancier's nuisance."

The Sheikh summoned his servant and instructed him to bring a long branch of a tree. When the slave had brought the branch, the Sheikh said to him: "Now take this branch to the pigeon-fancier and ask him not to throw stones but to use this instead to make the pigeons fly."[127]

2 – Tolerance Towards the Commander's Deeds

While Hishām Ibn Ismāʿīl (the maternal uncle of ʿAbdul Mālik Ibn Marwān) was the governor of Madinah, having been appointed by Yazīd, he used to harass Imām Sajjād عليه السلام immensely. When he was dismissed from the post, Walīd took his place, ordered him to be arrested and placed him in custody so that all those people who had grievances against him could come forward and seek compensation.

[126] Tadhkeratul Ḥaqāiq, Page 54
[127] Namunah-e-Maʿarif, Volume 4, Page 368

Hishām said, "I do not fear anyone except ʿAlī Ibn al-Ḥusain ﷺ." This fear was because he had subjected the Imām ﷺ to enormous troubles.

However, the Imām ﷺ had instructed some of the individuals known to him (and who had had a hand in Hishām's arrest) not to cause any harm to him, even by using a bad word. He even sent a message to Hishām stating: "Listen, if you are unable to pay the money which they have imposed upon you as penalty and punishment, we can arrange to have it paid for you. Rest assured! You need not be worried, either with respect to us or with respect to our followers."

When Hishām realised the Imām's civility and courteousness towards him in spite of his improper conduct, he recited aloud[128]: "Allāh knows best where He places His message."[129]

3 – Qais Minqarī

A narrator says: "I learnt to practice forbearance from Qais Ibn ʿĀsim Minqarī. Once, I watched him preaching and exhorting the people as he leaned on his sword in front of his house. In the course of his preaching, I observed that some people came to him with a dead body together with a person whose hands were tied.

"This is your nephew and he has killed your son," they said to Qais.

The narrator continues: "By Allāh! Qais neither discontinued his speech nor did he get up from his place. Instead, he continued till his speech finished, after which, he turned to his nephew and said: "O' Nephew! You have committed an evil deed, disobeyed your Lord, severed your relationship, used your weapon to your own detriment and dishonoured the people of your tribe!"

---

[128] Noble Qur'an, Sūratul Anʿām (6), Verse 124

[129] Bā Mardum In Guneh Barkhord Konīm, Page 22; Tārīkh Tabarī, Volume 8, Page 61

Then, turning to his other son, he said: "Untie the hands of your cousin, bury your brother and give your mother, from my property, a hundred camels as blood money for the death of your brother, for she comes from a different family."[130]

4 – Imām Ḥasan and the Syrian

One day, Imām Ḥasan ﷺ was sitting in his place when he was confronted by a man who had come from Syria. As soon as the man set his eyes upon the Imām ﷺ, he began to curse and revile him; but the Imām ﷺ remained silent till he had completed his outburst.

When he had stopped, the Imām ﷺ turned towards him, greeted him, smiled and then said: "Brother! You seem to be a stranger here and you have apparently made a mistake. If you want me to disregard your behaviour and forgive you, I shall do so; if you seek something from me, I shall grant it to you; if you want me to guide you, I shall do so; if you are hungry, I shall feed you; if you are in need of clothes, I shall provide them to you; if you are needy, I shall give you all that you need; if you have been expelled, I shall grant you shelter and if you have a desire, I shall fulfill it for you. If you can be my guest for the duration of your stay here, it would be to your benefit, since my house is large and contains all amenities."

Hearing these words of Imām Ḥasan ﷺ, the man burst into tears and said: "I bear witness that you are Allāh's Caliph upon the earth and Allāh knows best where He places His message and caliphate. Before this meeting of ours, I regarded you and your father as my greatest enemies amongst the people, but now you are the most beloved of them all for me."

---

[130] Payghambar Wa Yārān, Volume 5, Page 180; Asad al-Ghābbah, Volume 4, Page 229

The man stayed with Imām Ḥasan ﷺ as his guest for the entire duration of his stay in Madinah and eventually became one of the sincere followers of the Ahlul Bayt.[131]

5 – Sheikh Ja'far Kāshif al-Ghitā

Sheikh Kāshif al-Ghitā was one of those illustrious scholars who were known to possess a high degree of forbearance.

One day, the Sheikh distributed some money amongst the impoverished people of the city of Iṣfahān after which he began to lead the congregational prayers. Between the two prayers, when the people were engaged in reciting their supplications, a poor sayyid[132] entered the mosque, stood before the Sheikh and shouted rudely: "O' Sheikh! Hand over the money of my grandfather (khums) to me."

"You have arrived late; unfortunately, I have nothing left with me," the Sheikh replied.

The sayyid, with great impertinence, spat on his beard!

Instead of reacting violently, the Sheikh spread out his cloak and began to walk amidst the rows of people, saying, "Whoever loves and respects the Sheikh's beard, should help this sayyid." The people, having witnessed what had transpired between the two, immediately obeyed and very soon the Sheikh's cloak was filled with money. He handed all the money to the sayyid and proceeded to lead the congregation for the 'Aṣr prayers.[133]

---

[131] Muntahal Ā'māl, Volume 1, Page 222

[132] A descendant of the Noble Prophet ﷺ. (Tr.)

[133] Seemā-e-Farzānegān, Page 338; Fawāid al-Raḍawiyyah, Page 74

35 – Modesty

Allāh, the Wise, has said:

﴿ إِنَّ ذٰلِكُمْ كَانَ يُؤْذِي النَّبِيَّ فَيَسْـــتَحْيِي مِنْكُمْ وَ اللّٰهُ لاَ يَسْتَحْــــيِي مِنَ الْحَقِّ ﴾

"Such (behaviour) annoys the Prophet: he is ashamed to dismiss you, but Allāh is not ashamed (to tell you) the truth."[134]

The Noble Prophet ﷺ said:

أَلْحَيَاءُ خَيْرٌ كُلُّهُ

"Every kind of modesty is goodness."[135]

Short Explanation

Modesty is a luminosity, the essence of which is faith, and therefore, modesty stems from faith and ought to be strengthened by means of it.

A person who possesses modesty enjoys every kind of goodness - restraining himself in the face of every repugnant and impure act - but one who lacks modesty and shame, acquires every kind of evil, although he may appear to engage himself in acts of worship. A person who lacks this virtue shall be left deprived (of mercy) and will be afflicted with the punishment of the Hereafter. Modesty, in the initial stage, transforms into 'fear of Allāh', while in the final stage, into 'perception of Allāh'.

A person who is in possession of this virtue, is heedful of Allāh, distant from sins and disobediences, and cloaked with honour and love.[136]

---

[134] Noble Qur'an, Sūratul Aḥzāb (33), Verse 53

[135] Jāmeʿ al-Saʿadāt, Volume 2, Page 385

1 – Mūsā and the Daughters of Shuʿaīb

When Mūsā عليه السلام killed the person from Qabt, the followers of Firʿawn schemed to have him murdered, and so he fled from Egypt. After travelling for between three and eight days and enduring great troubles, he reached the city of Madyan, where he stretched out to rest beneath a tree situated near a well.

He realized that there were two ladies standing near the well, waiting for the shepherds to finish drawing water so they too could draw water from the well. He went to them and offered to help by drawing the water for them. As a result of Mūsā's help, the women brought the water home sooner than usual and this prompted their father, Shoʿaib عليه السلام to inquire: "How did you manage to bring the water sooner than usual today?"

They narrated to him the entire episode, whereupon Sho'aib said, "Go to the man and bring him to me in order that I may reward him for his act."

The ladies approached Mūsā عليه السلام. As soon as they conveyed their father's message to him, he immediately agreed, as he was hungry, tired and a stranger in the place. The maidens led the way while Mūsā عليه السلام followed them, but as they walked, the outlines of their bodies became visible and this appeared unsuitable to Mūsā's modesty (to look at). Consequently, he said to them: "I shall lead the way while you follow up behind me; correct me if you find me heading in the wrong direction (or throw pebbles before me so that I know where to go) for we, the children of Yaʿqūb, do not look at the backs of women."

When the ladies approached Shoʿaib عليه السلام and related the incident to him, he gave his daughter in marriage to Mūsā عليه السلام, owing to the

[136] Tadhkeratul Ḥaqāiq, Page 93

latter's assistance, modesty, purity, trustworthiness and physical strength.[137]

2 - The Modesty of the Eyes

It has been related in the commentary Rūḥul Bayān that in a city there lived three brothers. The eldest brother had been the muezzin of the mosque in the city and used to recite the adhān from the top of its minaret. After extending his services for ten years, he died and the second brother took over his brother's task. A few years later, this brother died too and so, the people approached the third brother and urged him to accept this responsibility and not to let the sound of adhān be terminated. But he flatly refused.

"We shall give you a large amount of money!" they said to him.

But he replied, "Even if you were to give me a hundred times more, I would not accept this task."

"Is the recitation of adhān an evil act?" they asked him.

"No, but I shall not recite it from the top of the minaret."

When they sought to know the reason for his refusal, he said, "This minaret is a place that has caused my two wretched brothers to die without faith. I was near my eldest brother when he was breathing his last and I desired to recite the Sūrat Yāsīn to ease the agony of his death, but he prohibited me from reciting it.

"The second brother too departed from the world in the same manner. In order to know the reason for this problem, Allāh graced me and I saw my eldest brother in my dream, in a state of chastisement. I said to him: 'I shall not leave you till you tell me what caused both of you to die without faith?' He said: 'Whenever we ascended the minaret, we would look at the womenfolk in the people's houses, without

[137] Tārīkh-e-Anbiyā, Volume 2, Page 65-71

shame and modesty. This act of ours used to engage our hearts and occupy our thoughts, leaving us neglectful and heedless of Allāh, and this is what has caused us to become wretched and earned for us an evil Hereafter.'"[138]

3 – Zulaikha

When Zulaikha followed Yūsuf to gratify herself and proposed to commit the sin, Yūsuf suddenly observed that she had covered something with a piece of cloth.

"What did you do?" he asked her.

"I have covered the face of the idol so that it does not watch me while I commit the sin," she replied.

Hearing this, Yūsuf said, "(If) you exhibit shyness and modesty before a stone that does not see, it is more befitting for me to exhibit shame and modesty before the One, Who sees and Who is aware of what is manifest about me and what is concealed within me."[139]

4 – The Modesty of Amirul Moʿminīn

The marriage formula between Imām ʿAlī عليه السلام and Hadhrat Zahrā عليها السلام had been recited in the year 2 AH, but the wedding ceremony took place only later (after one month or one year, as per varying reports).

During this period, ʿAlī عليه السلام, out of shyness, would not utter the name of Fāṭimah عليها السلام and she too behaved likewise.

This continued till one day, the wives of the Noble Prophet ﷺ approached ʿAlī عليه السلام and asked: "Why do you delay the wedding ceremony? If you experience a feeling of shyness and timidity, permit

---

138 Riwāyat-hā Wa Hikāyat-hā, Page 105; Dāstān-ha-e-Parākandeh, Volume 1, Page 123

139 Namunah-e-Maʿarif, Volume 4, Page 385; Baḥrul Maḥajjah (of *Ghazzāli)*, Page 94

us to speak to the Noble Prophet ﷺ about it." Imām ʿAlī عليه السلام granted them permission.

En masse, they arrived in the presence of the Noble Prophet ﷺ.

"O' Prophet of Allāh!" they said. "Had Khadījah been alive, Fāṭimah's wedding ceremony would have left her overjoyed and Fāṭimah عليها السلام herself would be happy to set her eyes upon her husband. ʿAlī عليه السلام too awaits his wife and we look forward to this joyous occasion."

Hearing Khadījah's name, tears welled up in the Noble Prophet's eyes. With a heave of sigh, he said, "Where is there the like of Khadījah...?" and then added, "But why did ʿAlī عليه السلام not approach me directly for this?"

The wives replied, "His modesty restrained him from doing so."

Hearing this, the Noble Prophet ﷺ directed them to make preparations for the wedding ceremony.[140]

[140] Fāṭimah al-Zahrā, Page 283

36 – Fear

Allāh, the Wise, has said:

﴿ وَادْعُوْهُ خَوْفاً وَّ طَمَعاً ﴾

"And call on Him fearing and hoping."[141]

The Noble Prophet ﷺ has said:

أَتَمُّكُمْ عَقْلاً أَشَدُّكُمْ خَوْفاً

"The most perfect and complete from amongst you in intellect is the one who is most fearful amongst you (of Allāh)."[142]

Short Explanation

Fear of Allāh is the sentinel of the heart; this is because a fearful person, by means of fear, remains mindful of Divine pleasure and soars to lofty heights. He witnesses the Divine threats and warnings, and thus refrains from deeds that are dictated by carnal and base desires.

A person who worships Allāh out of His fear never gets deviated and eventually reaches his goal and objective. How can he afford not to be fearful especially since he does not possess knowledge of what his final outcome would be and is unaware if his Book of Deeds would be light or heavy?

A fearful person finds himself torn between two fears - fear of the past and that of the future. Fear serves to suppress one's (reckless) soul and when a person's soul is suppressed with respect to carnal and capricious desires, his heart comes to life. This leads to steadfastness,

[141] Noble Qur'an, Sūratul Āʿrāf (7), Verse 56
[142] Jāmeʿ al-Saʿadāt, Volume 1, Page 225

which eventually prepares the ground for the heart to develop hope and become hopeful (of divine mercy).[143]

1 - The Fearful Youth

Salmān Fārsī was passing through the blacksmiths' market of Kufah when he observed that a crowd had gathered around a youth who lay on the ground, senseless. When the people saw Salmān, they requested him to recite a supplication so that the youth could come out of his unconsciousness.

As soon as Salmān came closer, the youth got up and said: "There is nothing wrong with me. It is just that I was passing through this market when I noticed the blacksmiths striking metal with their iron hammer and this made me recall what Allāh has said in the Qur'an: "In addition there will be maces of iron (to punish) them."[144] As this verse crossed my mind, I was overcome by this state."

Salmān became interested in the youth, grew fond of him and made him his brother. They were always friends with each other till one day the youth fell ill and was almost on the verge of dying. Salmān sat down near his head and then, addressing Izrā'eel, said: "O' Izrā'eel! Be tolerant and lenient towards my young brother and be kind and gentle to him!"

"O' Servant of Allāh! I am the friend of all the believers and kind to them all," Izrā'īl replied.[145]

2 - The Mute Language of the Stone

It has been reported that once in the course of his journey, one of the Prophets came across a small stone and observed that a large quantity

---

[143] Tadhkeratul Ḥaqāiq, Page 83

[144] لَهُم مَقَامِعُ مِن حَدِيد (Noble Qur'an, Sūratul Ḥajj (22), Verse 21)

[145] Dāstān-e-Jawānān, Page 94

of water flowed out from it. As the incident left him greatly astonished, Allāh made speech come out from the stone, which said: “Ever since I heard that men and stones would be the fuel of the fire of Hell, I have been in a state of weeping (out of fear that I should be one of those stones).”

The stone then requested the Prophet to pray that it should remain protected from the fire (of Hell) and the Prophet, acceding to his request, prayed for it.

It so happened that after a period, the Prophet again passed by that place and, witnessing that the water still continued to flow from the stone as before, inquired: “What is it that makes you weep now?’

The stone replied, “Before I could be satisfied of my deliverance from the fire (of Hell), my tears were out of fear, but now, I weep out of thanksgiving and due to joy and happiness.”[146]

3 – Punishment by Fire

Once, Amīrul Mo’minīn عليه السلام was in the company of his companions when a person approached him and said: “O’ Amīrul Mo’minīn عليه السلام! Purify me for I have committed sodomy with a boy.”

“Go home for you appear to have been affected by bile or melancholia,” advised the Imām عليه السلام.

The next day the person turned up again and confessed to his dirty act but the Imām عليه السلام repeated what he had previously stated. The third day too he confessed and again Imām ʿAlī عليه السلام repeated his earlier advice. When the man arrived on the fourth day and confessed to his crime, the Imām عليه السلام said: “Now that you have confessed four times, choose one of the three punishments, which the Noble Prophet صلى الله عليه وآله has stipulated for this act – to be beheaded by means of a sword, to be

[146] Shanīdani-hā-e Tārīkh, Page 388; Maḥajjatul Baiḍā, Volume 7, Page 142

hurled down from a height or to be burned with your hands and feet tied."

"Which of these three punishments would be the severest for me?" the man asked.

"Burning by fire."

"O' ʿAlī! عليه السلام, I choose this punishment."

The Imām عليه السلام told him to prepare for it. The man got up, offered a two-rak'at prayer and supplicated: "O' Lord! I have committed sin and You are aware of it. Fearing Your wrath, I have approached the successor and the cousin of the Noble Prophet ﷺ and have asked him to purify me of it. He asked me to choose one of the three punishments and I have chosen the most severe one. O' Lord! I plead to You by Your mercy to make my burning in this world an expiation for my sin and not to burn me in the Hereafter!"

Having said this, he got up, began to weep and then hurled himself into the pit of roaring flames. The Imām عليه السلام began to weep when he saw this and so did his companions; then he said in a loud voice: "O' Man! Rise from within the fire for you have caused the angels to weep. Allāh has accepted your repentance. Rise and henceforth do not conduct such an act!"

It is reported in another tradition that a person asked ʿAlī عليه السلام, "O' Amīrul Mo'minīn عليه السلام! Do you invalidate the punishment of Allāh?"

Imām ʿAlī عليه السلام replied, "Woe unto you! Whenever there exists an Imām appointed by Allāh and a sinner repents for his sin, it is upon Allāh to forgive him."[147]

---

[147] Dāstān-hā-e-Zindagi-e-ʿAli عليه السلام, Page 51; Qadhāwat-hā-e-Muhayyir al-ʿUqūl

4 – The Fearful Ones

When the verse: "And surely Hell is the promised place of them all. It has seven gates; for every gate there shall be a separate party of them"[148] was revealed to the Noble Prophet ﷺ, he wept so intensely that it made his companions weep too, but none knew what it was that Jibra'īl had revealed which had made the Noble Prophet ﷺ wail in such a fashion.

One of the companions went to Fāṭimah عليها السلام and informed her of the incident. Covering herself with her cloak, which was patched in twelve places by means of date palm leaves, she came out of the house. When Salmān Fārsī's eyes fell upon the cloak, he looked at it in amazement and then, bursting into tears, said to himself: "The emperors of Rome and Iran attire themselves in silken and gold-embroidered clothes but the daughter of the Noble Prophet ﷺ covers herself with such a cloak!"

When Fāṭimah عليها السلام came to the Noble Prophet ﷺ, he said to Salmān: "My daughter belongs to a group that has taken great precedence in subservience and obedience (to Allāh)."

Fāṭimah عليها السلام then asked, "Father! What was it that made you grieve?"

The Noble Prophet ﷺ recited the verses which had been brought by Jibra'īl. The mention of Hell and the punishment of the fire left her so distraught that her knees failed to hold her weight and she collapsed onto the floor saying, "Woe unto he who enters the fire."

"O' I wish I had been a sheep that was eaten and my skin had been torn apart so that I would never have had to hear of the fire of Hell," uttered Salmān.

---

148 وَ اِنَّ جَهَنَّمَ لَمَوعِدُهُم اَجمَعِينَ لَهَا سَبعَةُ اَبوَابٍ لِكُلِّ بَابٍ مِنهُم جُزْءٌ مَقسُومٌ (Noble Qur'an, Sūratul Ḥijr (15), Verse 43-44)

"O' I wish my mother had never given birth to me so that I would never have heard of the Hell-fire," said Abū Dharr.

"I wish I was a bird in the desert so that I would not have had Reckoning nor punishment, and would not have heard of the fire of Hell," muttered Miqdād.

Amīrul Mo'minīn ﷺ said, "I wish the wild animals had torn me into pieces and my mother had not given birth to me so that I would not have had to hear of the Hell-fire." Then, placing his hand upon his head, he began to cry and wailed, "Oh! How distant is the journey of the Day of Judgment! Woe to those who did not make provision for the Day of Judgement. In this journey of the Day of Judgment, they shall be led towards the fire; O' the sick ones, who shall be in the binds of captivity and whose injuries shall never be treated. None shall step forward to untie them; fire shall be their food and water, and they shall be turned upside down in the various stations of Hell."[149]

5 – Yaḥyā

When Prophet Yaḥyā ﷺ observed the clerics of Baytul Maqdas wearing veils made of haircloth and headgears of cotton, he requested his mother to make a similar dress for him. Later, he began worshipping with them in Baytul Maqdas.

One day, Yaḥyā ﷺ looked at his body, which had become considerably thin, and began to weep. Allāh revealed to him: "You cry over your body that has thinned down? By My Glory and Majesty! Had you possessed the slightest knowledge of the fire (of Hell), you would have worn overcoats made of iron, not these woven clothes." Hearing this, Yaḥyā wept to such an extent that the flesh of his cheeks became worn out.

[149] Pand-e-Tārīkh, Volume 4, Page 221; Biḥārul Anwār, Volume 10, Page 26

Zakariyya ﵇ said to his son, "I had sought you from Allāh so that you could be the apple of my eyes. Why do you behave in such a manner?"

"Father, but was it not you who had said: 'Surely, between Paradise and Hell there lies a pass and none except those who cry immensely due to fear of Allāh, shall be able to traverse it'," Yaḥyā replied.

"Yes, I did!," admitted Zakariyya ﵇.

Whenever Zakariyya ﵇ intended to preach and exhort the Banī Isrāʾīl, he would first look around him, and if he noticed Yaḥyā ﵇ amongst them, he would refrain from mentioning anything about Paradise and Hell. Once, Zakariyya ﵇ was engaged in delivering a sermon to the people when Yaḥyā ﵇, his head covered with his cloak, arrived and sat down amongst the people. Zakariyya ﵇, who had not noticed Yaḥyā ﵇, preached: "Allāh has said: 'In Hell there is a mountain by the name of Sakarān alongside which there lies a desert by the name of Ghadhabān, in which there is a well whose depth is equivalent to one hundred years of travel. Within this well, there exist caskets of fire and within these caskets lie chests of fire, which in turn contain clothes and chains of fire."

As soon as Yaḥyā ﵇ heard the name 'Sakarān', he raised his head, shrieked and in a state of utter distress and disturbance, rushed out and headed towards the wilderness.

Zakariyya and Yaḥyā's mother set off in search of him; some of the youths of Banī Isrāʾīl too, out of respect for Yaḥyā's mother joined them in their search. They came across a shepherd and asked him if he had seen a youth with Yaḥyā's description.

"Are you looking for Yaḥyā Ibn Zakariyya?" inquired the shepherd.

"Yes," they replied.

"He is presently in a particular place with his feet in the water and his eyes glued towards the heavens, praying and communicating with his Lord," he explained.

The search party went to that place and located him. Calling Yaḥyā عليه السلام towards herself, his mother placed him under the oath of Allāh and requested him to return home. Soon, Yaḥyā عليه السلام returned home with his mother.[150]

[150] Risālah Liqāullāh, Page 157-164; Amāli of al-Ṣaduq

37 – Treachery

Allāh, the Wise, has said:

﴿ إِنَّ اللّٰهَ لاَ يُحِبُّ مَنْ كَانَ خَوَّاناً أَثِيْماً ﴾

"Surely Allāh does not love him who is treacherous, sinful."[151]

Imām Ṣādiq عليه السلام said:

لَيْسَ لَكَ أَنْ تَأْتَمِنَ الْخَائِنُ

"It is not for you to trust a treacherous person."[152]

Short Explanation

If a thing such as money, a business, a car or the like is placed as trust in one's possession, one should not be unfaithful to it, spoil or disfigure it or deny having received it as a trust.

A person with this vice does not have credibility neither in the eyes of Allāh nor in the eyes of the people. He drops down from the level of faith and the (evil) reaction of his deed rebounds – affecting him, his wealth and his family in a detrimental way.

It has been strongly advised that one should not be deceived by a person's (prolonged) prayers and (numerous) fasts - for it is possible that the person may have simply become fond of performing these acts – instead, one should test a person for truthfulness, and faithfulness with respect to the trusts (placed in his custody).

One should never place a trust in the possession of an unfaithful person. Lending money or giving one's daughter in marriage to a treacherous person is disapproved and if one does so and then

[151] Noble Qur'an, Sūratul Nisā (4), Verse 107

[152] Biḥārul Anwār, Volume 78, Page 248

happens to suffer loss or harm, it is only himself that he should censure and rebuke.

1 – The Treacherous Minister

During his reign, Gushtasp had a minister by the name of Rāst Rawishan[153]. As a result of this prestigious name, Gushtasp held him in high esteem and favored him over the other ministers.

This minister exhorted Gushtasp into oppressing the subjects and confiscating their property in the belief that the orderliness of the kingdom's affairs was dependent upon the treasury and that the subjects ought to be poor in order that they remained subservient and obedient. He himself had not only accumulated a lot of wealth but had come to harbour animosity towards Gushtasp.

One day, when Gushtasp came to the treasury, he realised that there was no money to pay his workers. Furthermore, his cities were falling into ruin and the people were in distress. This left Gushtasp in a state of bewilderment.

Out of sheer despair, he climbed onto his horse and set off into the wilderness. As he wandered, his eyes fell upon a flock of sheep in the distance. When he came nearer, he observed that the sheep were sleeping while a dog lay suspended from the gallows. In astonishment, he asked the shepherd the reason for killing the dog. The shepherd replied: "This dog was a loyal animal; I nurtured him and trusted him to protect the sheep. After a period, he came in contact with a she-wolf and both became friends. When night fell, the she-wolf would take hold of a sheep, eat half of it, and leave the other half for the dog.

"One day, I noticed a decrease in the number of sheep and after investigation, came to know of the dog's treachery. Therefore, I hung

[153] Literally, his name means 'a truthful worker'.

him up on the gallows so that it is known that the consequence of treachery and evil is torture and punishment!"

Hearing this, Gushtasp thought to himself, "My subjects are like these sheep and I am like the shepherd; I must investigate and study the condition of the people so that I know the cause for their deplorable state."

He returned to his court and asked for the list of prisoners who were locked in his prisons. Studying the list, he concluded that his minister, Rāst Rawishan, had imprisoned all of them and that he was the cause of all the evils and troubles. He had the minister hanged and admitted to himself that he had been deceived by his name.

Gradually he made the kingdom prosperous, rectified the past damages, paid attention to the state of the captives and refrained from trusting anyone, ever again.[154]

2 – Treachery during Ziarat

Al-Hājj Ḥasan, the son of Āyatullāh al-Hājj Ḥusain Ṭabāṭabā'ī Qummī, relates: "I had come to Tehran from Mashhad for the treatment of my eyes. During that time, one of the traders of Tehran who was known to me, had travelled to Khurasan for the ziārat of Imam Riḍā عليه السلام.

One night, I dreamt that I was in the sanctuary of Imām Riḍā عليه السلام who was seated on the sepulcher. Suddenly, I observed that the trader shot an arrow at the Imām عليه السلام which greatly troubled him. For the second time, from another direction of the sepulcher, he let fly another arrow towards the Imām عليه السلام and again the Imām عليه السلام was deeply troubled. The third time, the trader shot an arrow from behind but on this occasion, the Imām عليه السلام collapsed on his back. Shocked and petrified, I woke up from my sleep.

[154] Jawāme' al-Hikāyāt, Page 313; Siyāsatnāmeh-e-Khwājah Nidhām al-Mulk

When my eye treatment was completed, I wished to go back to Khorasan but then decided to stay on till the trader returned from Khorasan. When he returned, I spoke to him and asked him certain questions but could not get to the bottom of the matter. Eventually, I narrated my dream to him, whereupon, with tears flowing from his eyes, he explained: "One day, having entered the sanctuary of Imām Riḍā ﷺ, I noticed that before me stood a lady with her hand placed on the sepulcher. I placed my hand on hers and so the lady went to the other side of the sepulcher. I followed her there and once again placed my hand on hers. This time, the lady went behind the sepulcher. When she had placed her hand upon it, I did exactly the same as before and asked her where she was from. She replied that she was from Tehran; we became friends and returned to Tehran together."[155]

3 – The Daughter's Disloyalty towards the Father

Sātrun, whose title was Dhīzan was the king of Hadhar, a state located between the rivers Tigris and Euphrates. In Hadhar, there was a beautiful palace by the name of Jausaq.

Once, the king attacked a city that was under the control of Shapur; looting and plundering it, he massacred a great number of its people and eventually occupied it. In the process he managed to take Shapur's sister as captive.

When Shapur came to know of this, he gathered his army and set out towards the king. Dhīzan had locked himself inside a strong fort which Shapur laid siege to. This siege continued for a period of four years but Shapur was unable to penetrate the fort.

---

[155] Rāhnama-e-Sa'adat, Volume 1, Page 257; Jāme' al-Durar, Volume 1, Page 448

One day, Dhīzan's daughter, Nadhīrah, an extremely beautiful maiden, was strolling outside the fort when Shapur's eyes fell on her. He was instantly captivated by her beauty. He sent word to her that if she helped him conquer the fort, he would marry her. During one of the nights, Nadhīrah, who too had fallen for Shapur, got the guards of the fort intoxicated and opened its doors to Shapur's forces. In the battle that ensued, her father Dhīzan was eventually killed.

In keeping with his promise, Shapur married Nadhīra. One night he noticed that there was blood on her bed. As he set about to investigate the cause of it, he observed that a strand of thick hair lay on her bed and this had caused her delicate and subtle body to become scratched and injured.

"What did your father feed you with?" he asked her.

"Yolk of eggs, brain of lambs, butter and honey," she replied.

When he heard this, Shapur reflected for a while and then said:

"Despite these comforts provided by your father, you were not loyal to him; how can you ever be loyal and faithful to me?"

He ordered that she be tied to a horse's tail and the animal made to gallop through the desert so that the desert thorns become coloured by the blood of this treacherous and unfaithful daughter.[156]

4 - The Indian and the Sixth Imām

Imām Kaẓim ﷺ narrates: "One day, I was with my father in the house when a friend entered and told my father that some people were standing outside, waiting to see him. My father asked me to find out who they were. As I went outside, I saw numerous camels laden with chests and a man seated on a horse.

"Who are you?" I asked the man.

---

[156] Namunah-e-Ma'ārif, Volume 5, Page 142, Al-Mustatraf, Volume 1, Page 210

"I am from India and seek the honour of meeting the Imām عليه السلام," he replied.

I returned to my father and informed him about the man outside.

"Don't let this impure and treacherous person enter the house," he instructed, and so I did as I was told. The people pitched their tents at that very place near the house and waited for a long time till Yazīd Ibn Sulaīmān and Muḥammad Ibn Sulaīmān intervened and procured permission for them to meet my father.

When the Indian entered, he sat down before the Imām عليه السلام with folded knees and said: "May you have good health! I am from India and the king has sent me with some presents which are to be handed over to you. For several days I have been seeking permission to enter but you have been refusing to meet me. Do the Prophets' children conduct themselves in this manner?"

My father عليه السلام lowered his head and answered, "You will come to know the reason for it later." He then asked me to open the letter that the Indian had brought. In the letter, the king of India had extended his greetings. Then he had written: "It is because of you that I have been guided aright. I had been presented with an extremely beautiful slave-girl, and I found none, save you who could be worthy of possessing her and so, in addition to some clothes, ornaments and perfumes, I gift her to you. Out of one thousand persons, I selected one hundred, and from them, I selected ten and from the ten, I have short listed one person, Mizān Ibn Khabbāb, who is trustworthy. I send him to you together with the slave-girl and the presents."

My father turned to the Indian and said, "O' Unfaithful person! Turn back, for I shall never accept a trust that has been subjected to unfaithfulness."

The Indian swore that he had not been unfaithful, however my father told him, "If your clothes were to testify that you had been unfaithful with respect to the slave-girl, would you become a Muslim?"

"Do forgive me!" implored Mizān.

"Then write your deeds to the king of India."

"If you know something in connection with the issue, you write it down," said Mizān.

The man had a sheepskin over his shoulder; the Imām ﷺ told him to place it on the ground.

My father then offered a two-rak'at prayer after which he went into prostration and supplicated:

أَللّٰهُمَّ إِنِّي أَسْـــئَـلُكَ بِمَعَاقِدِ الْعِزِّ... إِيْمَانًا مَعَ إِيْمَانِهِمْ

then raising his head, he turned towards the sheepskin and said:

"Speak out all that you know about this Indian."

The sheepskin began to speak as if it were a sheep, and said:

"O' Son of the Prophet of Allāh! The king considered this person to be trustworthy and had laid great emphasis with regards to protecting the slave-girl and the gifts. When we had travelled some distance, we reached a desert where heavy rains lashed us. All our belongings had become soaked due to the rain. A short while later the clouds cleared away and the sun began to shine. At that point, this unfaithful person called out to the servant, who had been accompanying the slave-girl, and dispatched him towards the city to purchase something. When the servant had gone, he said to the slave-girl: "Enter into this tent which we have pitched beneath the sun so that your clothes and body dry up. The slave-girl entered the tent and pulled up her clothes up to her calves. As soon as his eyes fell upon her legs, he became mesmerized and persuaded the slave-girl into being unfaithful."

The Indian, disturbed and distressed at witnessing the sheepskin (speaking out his misdeed), confessed to his misdemeanour and sought forgiveness. The sheepskin returned to its original state and the Imām عليه السلام ordered him to put it on. As soon as the Indian had placed it over his shoulder, it encircled and tightened itself around his neck and the man was almost on the verge of being strangulated when the Imām عليه السلام said: "O' Sheepskin! Leave him so that he can return to the king who would be the most appropriate person to punish this man for his unfaithfulness."

The sheepskin reverted back to its original state. The Indian, overcome with fright, implored the Imām عليه السلام to accept the gifts.

"If you become a Muslim, I shall gift the slave-girl to you," said the Imām عليه السلام.

But he declined the offer. The Imām عليه السلام then accepted the presents, but refused to take the slave-girl, and the man returned to India.

After a month, a letter arrived from the king of India, in which, after extending his greetings he wrote: "You accepted that which did not have any significant value, whereas rejected that which was valuable. This left me greatly disturbed and I said to myself: 'The children of the Prophets possess divine insight and wisdom and it is possible that the person who had escorted the slave-girl, might have exhibited unfaithfulness.' And so, I wrote a letter in your name to myself, and said to the man that your letter had reached me in which you had mentioned his unfaithfulness. I said to him: 'Nothing, except the truth, can save you', whereupon he confessed and related to me the entire episode of his unfaithfulness with regards to the slave-girl and the incident of the sheepskin. The slave-girl also confessed and so I ordered both of them to be beheaded.

"I bear witness to the Unity of Allāh and the Prophethood of the Noble Prophet ﷺ and have to state that I shall personally arrive in your presence later."

Before long, he arrived in Madinah after having abdicated his kingship and transformed himself into a true Muslim.[157]

[157] Pand-e-Tārīkh, Volume 1, Page 217; Biḥārul Anwār, Volume 11, Page 136

38 – The World

Allāh, the Wise, has said:

﴿ وَ مَا الْحَيَاةُ الدُّنْيَا إِلاَّ لَعِبٌ وَّ لَهْوٌ ﴾

"And this world's life is naught but a play and an idle sport."[158]

The Noble Prophet ﷺ stated:

مَنْ أَصبَحَ وَ الدُّنْيَا أَكْبَرُ هَمِّهِ فَلَيْسَ مِنَ اللهِ فِي شَيْءٍ

"He who rises in the morning such that his greatest concern is for (the issues of) the world, shall have nothing of (the guardianship) of Allāh."[159]

Short Explanation

The world is like a figure whose head is pride; its eyes, greed; its ears, covetousness; its tongue, dissimulation; its hands, lust; its legs, vanity and its heart, heedlessness. Whoever loves the world, will be dragged by it towards arrogance and pride; whoever likes the world, will be made greedy by it towards itself and whoever desires the world, will be hauled by it towards covetousness.

A person who has praised the world has cloaked himself with the garment of dissimulation; one whose goal and objective is this world, his heart gets filled with vanity, and one who trusts this world, is overcome by negligence and heedlessness (with respect to Allāh). Consequently, Hell shall be the abode of the worldly people.[160]

---

[158] Noble Qur'an, Sūratul Anʿām (6), Verse 32

[159] Jāmeʿ al-Saʿadāt, Volume 2, Page 24

[160] Tadhkeratul Ḥaqāiq, Page 35

1 – Esteem and Humiliation

Hārūn Rashīd, the ʿAbbāsid Caliph, was very fond of the Barmaki family. They were his close and special companions, generally occupying ministerial posts, and from amongst them, he was particularly fond of Jaʿfar Barmakī. This mutual respect and esteem continued for over 17 years. In 189 AH, due to certain events, the Barmaki family became the object of Hārūn's wrath and consequently, all of them went through very difficult times.

Muḥammad Ibn ʿAbdul Raḥmān Hāshmī narrates: "On the day of ʿEīdul Adhā, I approached my mother who was having a conversation with a lady dressed in old clothes.

"Do you recognize this lady?" my mother asked me. I said I did not.

"This is ʾUbādah, the mother of Jaʿfar Barmakī," she said.

I moved towards ʿUbādah and spoke to her for sometime, all the while experiencing astonishment over the state she was in.

"O' My Mother! What have you seen of the wonders of the world?" I asked her.

ʿUbādah replied, "O' Son! I have experienced a day of ʿEīd, similar to this day (ʿEīdul Adhā), when I had four hundred slave-girls standing before me at my service and (yet) I used to complain that my son Jaʿfar had not granted me my right (fully) for I should have had more slave-girls serving me. Today is another day of ʿEīd but I am now faced with a situation in which the only things I require are two sheepskins - one for use as a mattress and the other for use as a blanket."

Muḥammad Hāshmī continued: "I gave her five hundred dirhams, which made her so happy that she almost died of delight. ʿUbādah kept coming to our house periodically, till she eventually passed away."[161]

---

[161] Tatimmah al-Muntahā, Page 181

2 – ʿAlī and the Public Treasury.

Shuʿbī narrates: "Accompanying the other youths, I too entered the vast open ground of Kufah where I saw Amīrul Mo'minīn عليه السلام holding a small whip in his hand and standing near two containers filled with gold and silver coins. He used the whip to keep back the huge crowd that had gathered whilst he was distributing the money.

The Imām عليه السلام continued to distribute the money till there was nothing left for himself, and he returned home empty-handed at which point, I went home too.

"I have witnessed a very strange thing today and I fail to comprehend if this person's act was good or bad, in that he never retained anything for himself!" I said to my father.

My father inquired as to what I was talking about. I narrated to him all that I had witnessed, whereupon my father, bursting out in tears, said to me: "Son, you have just watched the most excellent person from amongst all the people." [162]

◈◈◈

Zadhān reports: "Qambar and I set off see Amīrul Mo'minīn عليه السلام. When we reached him, Qambar said: "O' Amīrul Mo'minīn! Arise, for I have concealed a significant treasure for you."

"What is the treasure?" inquired the Imām عليه السلام.

"Arise and accompany me in order that I show it to you," insisted Qambar.

The Imām عليه السلام got up and followed him into the house. Qambar brought out a linen bag, which was full of small sacs containing gold and silver coins.

[162] Al-Ghārāt, Volume 1, Page 55; Dastān-hāi Az Zindagi ʿAlī عليه السلام, Page 114

"O' Ali! I know that you distribute everything amongst the people and never retain anything for yourself and so, I have saved this especially for you!" said Qambar.

Imām ﷺ remarked, "I would have preferred you to set this house on fire and burn down everything." As he said this, he struck the bag with his sword, causing the gold and silver coins to fall out. He then ordered us to distribute the coins among the people. After we had carried out his instructions, the Imām ﷺ said: "Bear witness that I have not taken anything for myself and have not been negligent with respect to the distribution of money amongst the Muslims. O' Gold and Silver! Deceive someone other than ʿAlī."[163]

3 – Hadhrat Sulaīmān

Sulaīmān Ibn Dāwūd ﷺ was one of those very few Prophets to whom Allāh had granted sovereignty over the east and the west of the world. For years, he ruled over jinn, men, animals, birds and wild beasts, and knew the language of all creatures - an authority so great and extensive that it was ineffable.

He had prayed to Allāh: "Grant me a kingdom the like of which You shall never grant to anyone after me."

After Allāh had graced and honoured him with such a kingdom, Hadhrat Sulaīmān ﷺ said to his servants one day: "I have not passed one single day, from morning to night, in a state of happiness. Tomorrow I shall enter my palace, climb onto its roof and view my subjects. Do not permit anyone to approach me lest my happiness should turn into sadness."

The next morning, taking hold of his staff, he climbed to the uppermost portion of his palace and stood there, leaning upon his

[163] Dastān-hāi Az Zindagi ʿAlī ﷺ, Page 128; Nahjul Balāgha (Ibn Abil Ḥadīd), Volume 8, Page 181

staff, observing his kingdom and subjects, and experiencing joy over what Allāh had granted to him. As he was looking around, he suddenly noticed a good-looking youth, dressed in clean clothes, appearing from one corner of his palace.

"Who granted you permission to enter the palace?" he asked the youth.

"The Lord," replied the youth.

"Who are you?" asked Sulaīmān عليه السلام.

"Izrā'īl."

"Why have you come?"

"To seize your soul, Sulaīmān."

"I had wanted today to be my day of happiness but Allāh desired otherwise; comply with the orders given to you," said Sulaīmān عليه السلام.

Izrā'īl seized his soul while he stood leaning on his staff while the people, looking at him from afar, thought him to be alive.

When time passed, there arose a controversy amongst the people. Some said, "It has been several days that he has not eaten or drunk anything and so he is our Allāh." Another group said, "He is a sorcerer; he has made it to appear to us that he stands, whereas, in reality, it is not so." A third group said, "He is a Prophet of Allāh."

Allāh sent an army of ants to eat through his staff as a result of which, the staff broke and Sulaīmān collapsed. It was then that the people realized that he had passed away several days before.[164]

4 - Ṭalhah And Zubaīr's Love for the World

Ṭalhah and Zubaīr had been of the elders during the initial phase of Islam and had extended fitting contributions in the battles. After the

[164] Ḥayāt al-Qulūb, Volume 1, Page 370

death of the Noble Prophet ﷺ, both of them, and Zubaīr in particular, vehemently supported Amīrul Mo'minīn ﵇ and never hesitated in offering their assistance to him.

Their support continued till ʿUthmān was murdered and the people selected Imām ʿAlī ﵇ as their leader. When this happened, these two approached Imām ﵇ and formally requested him to appoint them as governors of some cities.

However, when they encountered a negative reply from Imām ʿAlī ﵇, they conveyed a harsh message to him through Muḥammad Ibn Ṭalhah, which said: "We have had to make a lot of sacrifices for the sake of your Caliphate and now that you have the reins of power in your hand, you act as a dictator, bringing to the fore the likes of Mālik Ashtar and pushing us into the background?!"

Imām ʿAlī ﵇ sent a message through Muḥammad Ibn Talhah saying: "What should I do in order that you may be pleased?"

"Appoint one of us as the governor of Baṣrah and the other as the governor of Kufah," they replied.

"By Allāh! When I do not consider them to be trustworthy here in this place (Madinah), how can I place them over the people of Baṣrah and Kufah?" asked Imām ʿAlī ﵇.

He then instructed Muḥammad Ibn Ṭalhah to go and tell them: "O' Sheikhs! Fear Allāh and His Prophet with respect to the ummah of the Noble Prophet ﷺ and do not oppress the Muslims; have you not heard Allāh say: "(As for) that future abode, We assign it to those who have no desire to exalt themselves in the earth nor to make mischief and the good end is for those who guard (against evil)."[165]

Having failed to realize their ambitions of power and riches, Ṭalhah and Zubaīr decided to go to Makkah. They approached Imām ʿAlī ﵇

[165] Noble Qur'an, Sūratul Qaṣaṣ (28), Verse 83

to seek his permission to go to Makkah for performing the ʿUmrah. The Imām ﷺ told them that they did not really intend to perform the ʿUmrah, but they swore that they had no other motive and were firm and faithful in their pledge of allegiance.

Upon the Imām's orders, they renewed their pledge with him and then set out for Makkah. There, they broke their pledge, raised an army and in the company of ʿĀishah, set out towards Baṣrah for the Battle of the Camel! On the way, they met Yaʿli Ibn Munabbah, who carried with him approximately four hundred thousand dinars for Imām ʿAlī ﷺ from Yemen.

The two men forcefully took away the money from him and utilized it for fighting the Imām ﷺ.

In this battle (36 AH), thirteen thousand soldiers from the army of Ṭalhah and Zubaīr and five thousand soldiers from Imām ʿAlī's ﷺ army were killed. Ṭalhah was eventually killed by an arrow shot by Marwan, who belonged to his own army. After killing him, Marwan declared: "I have extracted revenge of 'Uthman's blood from Ṭalhah."

Zubaīr withdrew from the battle and was murdered on the way by Ibn Jurmuz. The consequence of their penchant for power and proclivity towards worldly desires was nothing but an ignominious death.[2]

5 - What he Desired and What Eventually Happened!

On the 23rd of Muharram, 169 AH, Mahdi ʿAbbāsi died in Māsabdhān and the caliphate passed on to his son Mūsā, titled Hadi ʿAbbāsi, who at that time, had gone to Jorjān to fight the people of Tabaristan.[3]

---

[2] Hikāyat-hā-e-Shanīdani, Volume 3, Page 20; Tārīkh-e-Yaʿqūbī, Volume 2, Page 169

[3] Modern day Māzandarān (Tr.)

Hārūn Rashīd, his brother, took the pledge of allegiance for him from the people of Māsabdhān and Baghdad and sent a message to inform him of the situation. Hadi quickly returned to the capital.

Harthamah Ibn A'ayun recounts: "One night, Hadi ʿAbbāsi summoned me to a private meeting with him.

"Do you know how disturbed I am because of this infidel dog Yaḥyā Ibn Khalid? He has turned the people against me and is coaxing them to support Hārūn. You must go to the prison immediately and behead him," he said. "Then proceed to the house of Hārūn and murder him. After this, survey the prison and kill every person from the progeny of Abū Ṭālib. When you have executed these instructions, prepare the army and proceed towards Kufah; once there, drive out all the descendants of ʿAbbās from their houses and set their houses on fire."

Hearing these instructions, a shiver ran through me.

"I do not have the strength to carry out these great and difficult tasks," I pleaded.

"If you exhibit negligence in obeying my orders, I shall kill you," he said, and ordered me to stand where I was whilst he went into the women's quarters.

I thought that since I had exhibited aversion towards these acts, he would assign them to someone else and then have me killed. I promised to myself that if I were delivered from this predicament, I would set off for a place where nobody would recognize me. Suddenly, a slave appeared and informed me that Hadi ʿAbbāsi had summoned me. Anticipating death, I testified to the Unity of Allāh and the Prophethood of the Noble Prophet ﷺ and advanced forward. Midway, I heard a lady speak out: "O' Harthamah! I am Khaizrān, Hadi's mother. Come and see what calamity has befallen us."

As I entered the room, Khaizrān, who was behind the curtains, said: "When Hadi entered the house, I moved aside the covering from my head and begged pardon for Hārūn, but he refused. At that moment he was suddenly overcome by a fit of severe coughing. He drank some water but it did not help and he died there and then (18 Rabi' al-Awwal, 170 AH). Now go and inform Yaḥyā Ibn Khalid of his death so that he can take the pledge of allegiance for my son Hārūn."

Harthamah continues: "I informed Yaḥyā of Hadi's death and then proceeded towards Hārūn's house, where I found him reciting the Noble Qur'an. I informed him that he had become the Caliph but he refused to believe it and so I narrated the entire incident to him. That very night, Hārūn was informed of the birth of his son, Mamun."[166]

---

[166] Rangārang, Volume 1, Page 24

39 – Lies

Allāh, the Wise, has said:

﴿ سَمَّاعُوْنَ لِلْكَذِبِ أَكَّالُونَ لِلسُّحْتِ ﴾

"(They are) listeners of falsehood, devourers of what is forbidden."[167]

Imām 'Askari ﷺ said:

جُعِلَتِ الْخَبَائِثُ كُلُّهَا فِي بَيْتٍ وَ جُعِلَتْ مِفْتَاحِهَا الْكِذْبُ

"All the evils have been placed in a house and lies have been made its key."[168]

Short Explanation

Speaking untruths - trivial or great, in jest or in seriousness - is not permitted since it has been said: "All the evils have been placed in a house and lies have been made its key", it becomes very important to abstain from this act.

Since lies refer to unrealities and one who utters lies, neither does so for the purpose of exaggerating his point nor for effecting reconciliation between two warring factions, it causes the angels to distance themselves from him. It brings about destruction of his faith, reduction in his livelihood, and humiliation and disgrace in the eyes of the people - to the extent that if untruths are ascribed to Allah and the Noble Prophet ﷺ in the month of Ramadhan, it even results in the invalidation of fasts.[169]

---

[167] Noble Qur'an, Sūratul Mā'idah (5), Verse 42
[168] Jāmeʿ al-Saʿadāt, Volume 2, Page 323
[169] Iḥyā al-Qulūb, Page 151

1 – Walīd Ibn 'Uqbah

Abi Mu'eet Walīd Ibn 'Uqbah was a Muslim who initially appeared to be such a righteous individual that the Noble Prophet ﷺ even assigned him the responsibility of collecting the zakāt and sadaqāt from the tribe of Banī Mustalaq. When the people of the tribe came to know of the arrival of a representative of the Noble Prophet ﷺ, they came forward to welcome him.

During the Age of Ignorance, there had existed enmity between Walīd and this tribe, and seeing the people come towards him in a large group, thought that they had prepared themselves to kill him. He quickly turned back and returned to Madinah.

He went to the Noble Prophet ﷺ, and told him that the people of the tribe were not willing to pay their zakāt, which obviously was not true.

The Noble Prophet ﷺ was upset to hear this and made up his mind to despatch an army towards the tribe, when Allāh revealed the following verse: "O you who believe! If an evil-doer comes to you with a report, look carefully into it[170](to ascertain the veracity of it)."[171]

After the revelation of this verse, the liar Walīd came to be recognized as a corrupt person.

"He is of the inmates of Hell," the Noble Prophet ﷺ said about him.

Walīd later teamed up with 'Amr Ibn 'Ās and the two would consume intoxicants and harboured feelings of animosity towards the Noble Prophet ﷺ and Amirul Mu'mineen عليه السلام.

The third caliph, during his caliphate, appointed him the governor of Kufah and one morning, in a state of intoxication, he led the morning

[170] Noble Qur'an, Sūratul Ḥujarāt (49), Verse 6 (يَا أَيُّهَا الَّذِينَ آمَنُوا إِن جَاءَكُمْ فَاسِقٌ بِنَبَإٍ فَتَبَيَّنُوا)

[171] Safīnatul Bihār, Volume 2, Page 361

congregational prayers by performing four-rak'ats instead of the stipulated two.[172]

2 – Hunger and Lies

Asmā Bint ʿUmais, reported: "On the night of ʿĀishah's marriage with the Noble Prophet ﷺ, a few ladies and I were with her, dressing her up. When we went to the house of the Noble Prophet ﷺ, we did not find any food except a single bowl of milk. He drank a little milk from it and then handed it to ʿAishah. Overcome by bashfulness, she did not take it.

"Do not refuse the Prophet of Allāh; take the bowl and drink the milk," I said to her. Shyly, she took the bowl and drank some milk from it.

"Pass on the bowl to your companions in order that they may drink from it too," the Noble Prophet ﷺ instructed her.

The ladies, who were with us, said, "We are not hungry."

Hearing this, the Noble Prophet ﷺ remarked, "Do not gather hunger and lies together (i.e. why do you lie while at the same time, you remain hungry?).

"O' Prophet of Allāh! If we were to possess an appetite for something but we deny having it, would we have uttered a lie?" I inquired.

"A lie, even if trivial and insignificant, is recorded in the Book of Deeds," stated the Noble Prophet ﷺ.[173]

3 – The Lies of the Poet

Khusro Hirawi was a contemporary of 'Abd al-Rahmān Jāmi, and the following verse is his composition: "The flower of your face has

---

[172] Ibid., Page 688

[173] Shanīdani-hā-e-Tārīkh, Page 294; Maḥajjatul Baiḍā, Volume 5, Page 249

watered the garden of beauty, and it has been the curls of your hair that have imparted the twists to the violets."

It has been reported that he said: "My father, who had prepared food on the occasion of my circumcision, had utilized three hundred kilograms of powdered saffron." Those present around him asked him what food he had put such a large quantity of saffron in.

"One hundred and twenty kilos in saffron-seasoned rice, ninety kilos in pea-soup, thirty kilos in fricassee and thirty kilos in sweat-meat," he replied.

"This sums up to two hundred and seventy kilos; what about the other thirty kilos?" his companions pointed out.

Bewildered, Khusro thought for a while after which he raised his head and lied with great exuberance: "I remember now. He used the final thirty kilos in 'quttāb'!" [174 and 175]

4 – Zainab the Great Liar

During the caliphate of Mutawakkil ʿAbbāsi, a woman claimed that she was Zainab, the daughter of Fāṭimah Al-Zahrā عليها السلام.

"Years have passed since the time of Zainab, but you appear to be young," said Mutawakkil to her.

"The Noble Prophet ﷺ caressed my head and prayed that every forty years I should become young again!" said the woman.

Mutawakkil called for the elders from the progeny of Abū Ṭālib, ʿAbbās and the Quraish and placed the issue before them. All of them unanimously averred that the woman was lying because Zainab had died in the year 62 AH.

[174] A sweetmeat (Tr.)

[175] Latāif al-Tawāif, Page 414

Zainab, the great liar retorted, "They are the ones who lie. I had concealed myself from the people and none knew of my whereabouts until today."

"You must establish the falsity of her claims by means of proofs," insisted Mutawakkil to the elders.

"Ask Imām Hadi عليه السلام to prove false her claims," they advised. Mutawakkil called for the Imām عليه السلام and informed him of the issue.

"She lies, for Zainab had died in such and such year," said the Imām عليه السلام.

"Present your evidence to prove false her claim," Mutawwakil demanded.

The Imām عليه السلام said, "The flesh of the children of Fāṭimah عليها السلام is forbidden upon the wild beasts; send her before the lions if she speaks the truth!"

Mutawakkil turned to the woman for an answer.

"In this way, he desires to kill me," said the woman.

"A number of people from the progeny of Fāṭimah عليها السلام are present here. You can send whoever you desire (before the wild beasts)," responded the Imām عليه السلام.

The narrator states: "The faces of all the sādāt present in the gathering turned pale. Some said, "Why does he not go himself instead of referring to others?"

Mutawakkil asked the Imām عليه السلام why he himself was not going before the lions. The Imām عليه السلام instantly agreed to go. Mutawakkil ordered for a ladder, and the Imām عليه السلام entered into the enclosure where the lions were maintained. The wild beasts, in submission and humility, placed their heads on the ground before the Imām عليه السلام and he in turn, caressed their heads. A little later he ordered them to move aside and all of them obeyed!

Mutawakkil's minister advised him, "Ask Imām Hadi ﷺ to come out immediately for if the people witness this miracle, all of them would flock to him."

The ladder was laid again and the Imām ﷺ climbed out.

"Whoever is of the children of Fāṭimah ﷺ should come forward and sit amongst the wild beasts," proclaimed Imām Hadi ﷺ.

The woman (having witnessed the scene) admitted, "O' Imām! My claims are false. I am the daughter of a certain destitute, and poverty forced me to resort to this deception."

Mutawakkil ordered his guards to throw the woman to the lions but his mother intervened and interceded for Zainab who was then pardoned."[176]

5 – The Plain Lie of Amir Ḥusain

Sultan Ḥusain Bāyaqra who ruled over Khorasan and Zabolistan, and Yaʿqūb Mirza who ruled over Azerbaijan, were friends who frequently sent letters and gifts to each other.

Once, Sultan Ḥusain handed over some exquisite and valuable items to a person named Amir Ḥusain Abyurdi and instructed him to pick the book 'Kulliyāt Jāmi' from the library and present it to Sultan Yaʿqūb Mirza along with the other items.

Amir Ḥusain approached the librarian and asked for the book, but the librarian erroneously handed him Muhyuddeen 'Arabi's book, Al-Futoohāt Al-Makkiyyah, which greatly resembled the book Kulliyāt Jāmi' in size and volume. Amir Ḥusain set out for Azerbaijan and arriving in Yaʿqūb Mirza's presence, handed him Sultan Ḥusain's letter and presents.

[176] Muntahal Aʿmāl, Volume 2, Page 368

After going through the contents of the letter, Yaʿqūb inquired after the health of Sultan Ḥusain and the other ministers of the Sultanate. He then asked about Amir Ḥusain's health and with reference to the long two-month journey that Amir Ḥusain had undertaken to reach him, he said: "You must surely have had a companion to make your journey pleasant."

"Yes, I had in my possession the book 'Kulliyāt Jāmi', which has been transcribed recently. Throughout the journey, I was engaged in reading it and thoroughly enjoyed it," replied Amir Ḥusain.

As soon as Yaʿqūb Mirza heard the name of Kulliyāt Jāmi', he said, "I had been desirous of this book and am extremely pleased that you have brought it." Amir Ḥusain sent one of his servants to bring the book and when it was brought, he handed it to Yaʿqūb Mirza. When Yaʿqūb Mirza opened the book, he observed that it was Al-Futoohāt Al-Makkiyyah. He turned to Amir Ḥusain and asked, "This is not Kulliyāt Jāmi' - why did you lie?"

Amir Ḥusain, embarrassed and ashamed, did not even wait to take the reply of the letter, but immediately set out for Khorasan.

"When my lie had been exposed, I wished that I had died," said Amir Ḥusain later on.[177]

---

[177] Khazīnatul Jawāhir, Page 640; Tārīkh Jaib al-Sair

40 – Theft

Allāh, the Wise, has said:

﴿ أَلسَّارِقُ وَ السَّارِقَةُ فَاقْطَعُوا أَيْدِيَهُمَا ﴾

"And (as for) the man who steals and the woman who steals, cut off their hands."[178]

Imām Ṣādiq عليه السلام:

إِذَا سَرَقَ السَّارِقُ قُطِعَتْ يَدُهُ وَ غُرِمَ مَا أَخَذَ

"When a thief commits a theft, his hands are cut and he is made to indemnify what he has taken."[179]

Short Explanation

Denying the wife her dower, not repaying one's debts, not paying one's obligatory zakāt and so on, are also examples of theft, but the meaning that immediately comes to mind upon hearing of theft, is 'taking into possession the property and wealth of others, secretly and deceptively' . This is the meaning which is actually intended here.

If there were to be no security (in the society), the people would be unable to sleep in peace for fear of thieves. It is for the purpose of establishing and maintaining security that Islam has ordered a thief's fingers to be severed; even if the act happens to be committed by a child, he has to be castigated in some manner, so that he desists from committing this evil act in the future.

It is due to the non-implementation of this Qur'anic ruling that an increasing number of thieves are found even in Islamic societies these days.

---

[178] Noble Qur'an, Sūratul Maidah (5), Verse 38

[179] Tafsīrul Mu'īn, Page 114

1 – The Imām and the Thief's Confession

A person approached Imām ʿAlī عليه السلام and confessed that he had committed a theft.

"Are you able to recite something from the Noble Qur'an?" Imām عليه السلام asked him.

"Yes, I know the chapter al-Baqarah," replied the man.

The Imām عليه السلام said, "I forgive you because of the chapter al-Baqarah." Ashʿath Ibn Qais, who happened to witness this, asked the Imām عليه السلام whether he could repeal a punishment that had been stipulated by Allāh.

"What do you know? If a person confesses to his crime, an Imām has the authority to either punish him or pardon him, but if two persons testify to a person's crime, it is not permissible to annul the punishment (and pardon him)," the Imām عليه السلام retorted.[180]

2 – The Bedouin's Camel

Sheikh Tawoos al-Haramain narrates: "I had been standing near Masjid al-Harām in Makkah when I witnessed a Bedouin advancing on his camel. When he reached the mosque, he dismounted, made his camel sit down, tied its two knees and then, raising his head towards the sky, implored: "O' Lord! I entrust unto You this camel and the load that lies upon it." Then he entered Masjid al-Harām. When he had circumambulated the Ka'bah and offered his prayers, he came out of the mosque and found his camel missing. He looked up towards the sky.

"It has been said in the holy Shari'ah that property should be sought from one, unto whom it has been placed as trust. I had entrusted my camel unto You, so return my camel to me," he said.

---

[180] Qadhawat-hā-e-Amirul Moʿminīn عليه السلام, Page 119 (authored by Tustari)

Hardly had he uttered these words when I observed that someone emerged from behind the mountain of Abū Qubais, with the rein of a camel in the left hand and the right hand severed and suspended from his neck. He came close to the Bedouin.

"O' Youth! Take hold of your camel," he said.

"Who are you and how did you land up in this state?" asked the Bedouin.

"I was impoverished and needy and hence stole your camel," said the stranger. "I went behind the mountain of Abū Qubais when I suddenly noticed a rider coming towards me. As he came closer to me, he shouted out: Bring your hand forward. When I had extended my hand, he severed it with a stroke of his sword and, hanging it on my neck, said to me: Return this camel to its owner immediately." [181]

3 - Buhūl and the Thief

Whenever Buhūl happened to have money in excess of his expenses, he used to save it by concealing it in one corner of a ruined and broken down house; this continued till the amount eventually reached a figure of three hundred dirhams.

The next occasion when he had saved another ten dirhams and had gone to the place to add it to his concealed savings, a trader who lived in the neighbourhood, found out about the hideout. As soon as Buhūl had left the hiding place, the neighbour dug up the money that was concealed beneath the ground.

The next time when Bulool came to the place, he found his money missing and immediately realized that it was the work of the trader. He decided to approach the trader.

[181] Rāhnama-e-Sa'ādat, Volume 2, Page 272; Khulāṣatul Akhbār, Page 526

"I wish to trouble you by telling you about my secret," Buhūl said to the trader. "I have placed my money in different places." Then he began enumerating the places till the entire figure reached three thousand dirhams. "The place where I have placed three hundred and ten dirhams is the safest of them all. I now wish to transfer all my money to this place in the ruined house." Saying this, he bid the trader goodbye and left.

The trader decided to return the three hundred and ten dirhams to the place from where he had stolen the money with the intention that when Buhūl placed all his money there, he would steal the increased amount. Some days later, Buhūl returned to the ruins and found the three hundred and ten dirhams in its original location. Taking out the money, he defecated there and covered it with earth.

Immediately after Buhūl had left, the trader rushed towards the spot and, removing the earth, sought to collect the entire money, only to find his hand dirtied by the excrement. He thus comprehended Buhūl's deception. A few days later Buhūl visited him.

"I want you to compute some figures associated with my money," said Buhūl. "How much does eighty dirhams added to fifty dirhams added to one hundred dirhams, and this sum added to the dirty odour that emanates from your hands, sum up to?"

Saying this, he took to his heels. The trader rushed after him in hot pursuit, but failed to catch him.[182]

4 – The Qur'an-Reciting Blind Thief

'Allām Ibn Al-Thamān says: "I was employed by a trader in Baṣrah when one day, I had to undertake a journey to 'Ubullah. I put five hundred dirhams in a bag and set out for the journey. I reached the banks of the river Tigris where I hired a boat. As I was passing by the

[182] Dāstān-hā Wa Pand-hā, Volume 2, Page 71; Khazāin Narāqi

region named Mismār, I noticed a blind person sitting by the riverbank, reciting the Qur'an. In a very sad voice, he called out: "O' Seaman! Take me in the boat for I fear that the animals might kill me at night." Initially the boatman refused but when I rebuked him, he consented. The blind man sat in the boat and continually recited the Qur'an from memory till we came near 'Ubullah, whereupon he stopped his recitation and began to disembark from the boat.

All of a sudden, I realized that the trader's money, which had been given to me in trust, was missing. Both the boatman and the blind person removed their clothes to prove that they had not taken the money. I thought to myself, "The trader is bound to kill me." Thousands of thoughts whirled in my mind and I began to weep and pray.

As I walked towards 'Ubullah, a man came up to me and sought to know the reason for my lamentations. I informed him of the theft of the trader's money.

"I shall show you a way (to extricate yourself from this problem)," he said. "Purchase some good food, go to the prison and plead to the prison warden to let you in. Inside the prison, go to Abū Bakr Naqqāsh and give him the food. He will inquire about your problem, and when he does so, narrate the entire story to him."

I followed his instructions and when I had narrated my problem to Abū Bakr Naqqāsh, he said: "Now proceed towards the tribe of Banī Hilāl and go to a certain house. Open the door and enter the house. There you will notice some handkerchiefs hanging behind the door. Tie one of them to your waist and sit down in a corner. A group of people will enter and engage themselves in consuming intoxicants; you should pick up a bowl too and after calling out, 'For the health of my (maternal) uncle, Abū Bakr Naqqāsh,' begin drinking from it. Upon hearing my name, they will inquire after my health. Pass this message to them: 'Yesterday, my nephew's money was stolen. Hand it back to him,' and they will hand over the money to you."

I did as instructed and they too, without any protest, handed over the bag of money to me. I requested them to inform me as to how the theft had taken place. After great reluctance, one of them asked me if I recognised him. Looking closely at him, I realized he was the same blind man who had been reciting the Qur'an, while the other person was the boatman.

"One of our associates swims underwater behind the boat," he explained. "When the Qur'an is recited, the traveller becomes so absorbed that he does not notice that we have thrown his money into the water. It is collected by the associate in the water and carried to the shore, to be distributed amongst ourselves when we gather together the next day. Today was the day for the distribution of the money, but since we have received orders from our chief, Abū Bakr Naqqāsh, we have returned the money to you."

I took possession of the money and thanked Allāh for having been delivered from this quandary.[183]

[183] Jawāmeʿ al-Hikāyāt, Page 357